for Mum, who taught me to be fierce, precise & persistent. To Koo Poh, for your industriousness & gnarled hands spent in service. Because of you I can MacGyver the crap out of any situation. for my Dad, who dared me to dream big & aim for the stars. To my bro, who showed me the ropes when I could only draw stick figures. To Joffy, for sharing a decade of love & life lessons.

WHAT I
COOK
when NOBODY'S WATCHING

POH LING YEOW

plum. Pan Macmillan Australia

CONTENTS

Introduction 6

SALTY

MUST KNOWS 13

SNACKISH 33

BOWL FOOD 59

PROPER QUICKIES 81

LONE RANGER 103

HANDMADE 121

CROWD PLEASERS 141

DEFO EURO 165

WANDERLUST 191

SWEETY

JAMFACE FAVES 215

COMFORT COMBOS 233

ASIAN FLAVES 245

SHOW STOPPERS 263

Thank you 280

Index 283

Introduction

A lot has happened since I started writing this book. The world is in metamorphosis and personally, I'm flying solo again. This has changed my relationship with the garden, ingredients, cooking, friends, my body, philosophies I've long held and even my dogs, Rhino and Tim. I'm focused on simplicity, gratitude, creating beauty and ritual in the mundane. Slowly, I'm daring to be the person I've dreamt of being – someone who is (mostly) confident and likes herself, someone who is searching to be defined by her own standards and not the expectations of others. It's both exhilarating and difficult, to be constantly challenging your own fears, to make a friend of uncertainty, but being brave is important if you truly desire growth.

The title of this book came from a fancy pot-luck dinner I went to, attended by a group of local chefs. When asked if the dish I brought to the table was something I made often, I guffawed and blurted out, 'No way, I only make things like this when people are watching!'. In tandem with this thought is a memory of reading the famous River Cafe cookbooks when I was just a novice cook. They are full of recipes that repetitively prescribe what I thought at the time to be the stupidly obvious trinity of olive oil, salt and pepper to any given protein or vegetable, and I vividly remember thinking, 'This is bollocks and NOT a recipe!'.

It's only taken me two decades, appreciating quality produce from my local farmers' market and growing my own food, to realise that olive oil, salt and pepper are really all you want when the ingredients are so close to perfection – perhaps a squeeze of lemon to enliven 'the buds' and create balance. It's about adding less and giving very few ingredients your undivided attention when heat is being applied, which gets me to my next point. Just promise me, when you flip through the book to not pooh-pooh recipes like Not-Boring Roasted Broccoli & Sweet Potato (see page 22), because I'll give you tips to take these simple ingredients to places you never have before!

As for the other stuff in the book, I'm skating pretty close to 50 and with this I feel qualified to impart some hard-earned wisdom – yup, it's time. So yes, this is part cookbook, part daggy DIY household tips and part 'Pohlosophies'. In short, I desperately want it to be useful and honest. I really hope this is the sort of book that gets sticky, scribbled on and dog eared, because living properly is messy.

I'll end by stating in very clear terms that I don't do any of the things I'm giving advice on brilliantly at all. I'm just trying like every other schmuck, because living with awareness, trying to manage the elusive work–life balance and simplifying is actually really hard, so go easy on yourself and remember that tomorrow is a new day!

Hugs,

Poh

COOK'S NOTES

You will notice that in the recipes in this book, timings are not always given, but perhaps a colour, texture or fragrance to aim for, and this is because more than anything I want this book to make you a confident cook. Learning to trust your instincts and senses, not just the cold hard clock, is the only way.

Different types of heat (electric, gas, induction), the pan surface (stainless steel, non-stick), the size of the pan and height of the sides will all affect the result and the length of time required. For instance, a pan with a large stainless steel surface and low sides will evaporate liquid much faster than one with a small surface and high sides, which tends to steam and retain moisture. Also, non-stick surfaces don't conduct heat as well, so are no good for sealing meat but great for custards and pancakes. For quick, intense heat you would use stainless steel or cast iron. Where aromatics should only soften but not colour, adding a good pinch of salt will help to delay the caramelisation. Whenever crushed garlic is to be sautéed, start with cold oil so you can be in complete control of how much the garlic is caramelised. Watch, smell, taste, listen, touch and FEEL your way ... I seem to have beginner's luck but don't be discouraged if a recipe doesn't quite work out the first time round. I've found that like life, it's when you make mistakes that you learn the most. Enjoy the adventure!

For those with dietary requirements, the recipes in this book have the below notations where applicable. Vegos and vegans, where the recipe is vegetable based, I trust you will know how to look after yourselves with appropriate substitutions, such as gelatine-free cream and plant-based milk. For coeliacs and people with a gluten intolerance, I'm assuming you will know to substitute wheat-based seasonings, such as soy sauce, with gluten-free alternatives, such as wheat-free soy or tamari.

GF – Gluten free

GFO – Gluten free option

DF – Dairy free

DFO – Dairy free option

V – Vegetarian

VO – Vegetarian option

VG – Vegan

VGO – Vegan option

Good luck & bon appétit!

NOT ASHAMED OF ...

1. Stock powder. For making instant stock if I don't have any homemade stuff in the freezer. A teaspoon can also be great for filling those hollow spots in a dish if it's just missing some umami depth.

2. Microwave rice. Being Chinese, the idea of this stuff used to horrify me, but the busyness of life finally broke me. Sometimes, it's little things like this that avert a meltdown.

3. Long-life milk for baking and cooking. It's so handy to have some in the pantry in case you run out of the fresh stuff. Also, milk powder, used with restraint, is great for helping to thicken sauces and homemade yoghurt before incubation.

4. Good-quality ready-made curry pastes. Look for styles of pastes made by brands from their country of origin.

5. Frozen fruit, peas and broad beans.

6. Tinned legumes, fruit and veg.

7. Microwaving nuts instead of roasting. Simply place the nuts in a bowl and microwave on high in 1-minute bursts until fragrant and lightly browned, but do stir them between bursts. For slivered or flaked nuts, be more attentive. They roast from the inside out so the best way to check is to cut into a nut. For finer nuts like slivered almonds, I would go 40-second bursts. For flavoured nuts, spritz them with water to dampen the surface then shake them in whatever spice and seasoning mix you want. Mix well to coat, then microwave as described above.

8. Freezing leftover hardy aromatics like chilli, ginger, galangal, lemongrass, makrut* lime leaves and curry leaves.

9. Enjoying Spam and instant noods.

10. Eating chocolate for breakfast.

*As the word kaffir is offensive in some cultures, I've chosen to use its alternative name.

SALTY

MUST KNOWS

Imperative for survival

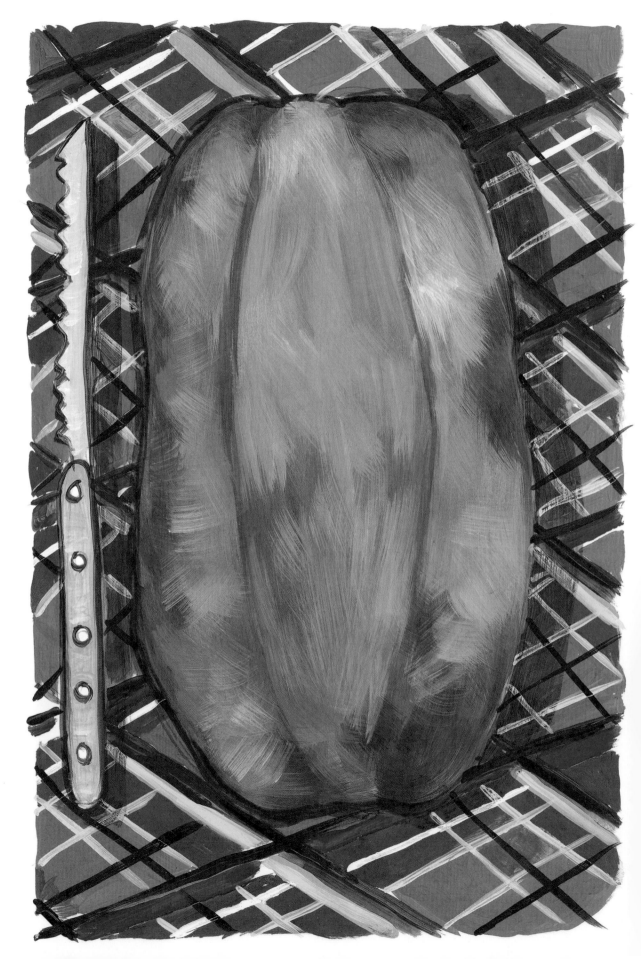

SOURDOUGH BREAD

I ummed and ahhed about including this recipe for the longest time because I knew the method was going to be so epic. I wasn't sure if you seeing such a dense block of text would render the exercise redundant. It's not that it's hard to do, what's difficult is describing things that are deeply rooted in instinct and touch. Once you develop a rhythm and an affinity with your starter, it will be like brushing your teeth and this is half the job.

My sourdough journey has been mostly self taught. I don't nerd out on moisture content ratios etc. I literally make it so I never have to buy terrible bread and have slowly edged my way to this result, making small adjustments from an original mother, method and recipe given to me in 2019 by *MasterChef* mate Reece Hignell. Also, sorry Reece, but I killed your mother recently.

You should know up front that you can't make pretty score marks for Instagram with this recipe because it has a very high moisture content – just one slash down the centre is all the dough will tolerate. A razorblade will work but a bread-slashing blade (lame) is best. They are incredibly thin and can be easily found in online cookware stores.

STARTER

60 g wholemeal flour

60 ml (¼ cup) tepid water, plus extra for feeding your starter

Plain bread flour, for feeding your starter

SOURDOUGH LOAF

About 300 g starter (see method)

600 g good-quality bread flour, plus extra if needed

400 ml tepid water, plus extra if needed

12 g salt

Rice flour, for dusting

MAKES 2 x ROUGHLY 700 G RUSTIC LOAVES

DF / VG

To make the starter, mix the wholemeal flour and water in a jar until you have a smooth, sticky paste. Secure cling wrap over the jar with an elastic band, then poke a few small holes in it and stand in a still spot for 3 days. If the weather is cold, a warmish spot, such as near an electrical appliance, is good, but otherwise an undraughty spot is fine.

After 3 days there should be evidence of bubbles. If there is brown liquid in the jar, tip it out before starting your first 'feed'. Measure out HALF (60 g) of the starter and discard the other half, then mix 60 ml (¼ cup) of water and 60 g of plain bread flour into it. Repeat this every day for 7 days.

On the seventh day you can make a loaf. This time, don't discard any starter, but add 180 ml of water and 180 g of flour and mix well. Measure 300 g of the starter into a large bowl or container and place the remaining 240 g of the starter in the fridge in a clear container or jar with a small hole in the lid – this is your 'mother' to keep feeding and making loaves from. This is the part where you find your rhythm. It's up to you how much starter you feed, and it will be based on how frequently you want to bake loaves.

Place the 300 g of starter in a warm spot to speed up the activation. It's useful to place a texta mark on the container so you can see the starter is rising. Once it's risen at least another half of its original height (I say at least because the height will vary according to the quality of activity in your starter and also the room temperature), scoop a teaspoon out and drop it in a glass of water. If it floats you're ready to go, but if it sinks, wait longer. Do not forge ahead or you'll wind up with a brick of a loaf!

SOURDOUGH BREAD (CONT.)

Once you get the go-ahead with the float test, place the starter, flour and water in the bowl of a stand mixer fitted with the dough hook attachment, and mix on the lowest speed for 3 minutes. Add the salt and mix for another 2 minutes. Raise the hook to inspect the dough – it should be glossy, smooth and sticking a tad to the base of the bowl. If not, you can add a tiny splash of water or a sprinkle of flour for the opposite issue, then mix for another minute.

Scrape down the side of the bowl, cover with a damp tea towel and sit in a warm spot.

After the dough has doubled in size (1–2 hours), wet your fingers to scoop under the edge of the dough, lifting and stretching it a little, then pushing it into the centre of the ball. Repeat all around the edge of the dough. Cover with the damp tea towel and allow to double in size again (1–2 hours).

Line two large baking trays with baking paper. Flour your workbench very well with rice flour before scraping the ball of dough out of the bowl and onto the bench. Using a serrated knife, very gently cut and tease apart the dough so you have two equal portions. Working with one portion at a time, gather the edge of the dough and pinch together in the middle to seal. Flip it smooth-side up, then nestle the opposite sides of the ball with both hands while gently shaping it into a more elongated loaf. Scoop it up swiftly with both hands and transfer to one of the prepared trays. Aim well and do it briskly because the dough has a high moisture content and will be very wobbly to handle. If it flattens, push the sides of your hands, palms facing up, into the dough to gently tuck the edge in. This will create some tension and keep the dough plump. Repeat with the second ball of dough, then cover with a damp tea towel to rise once more.

Meanwhile, preheat the oven to 250°C fan-forced.

When the loaves have almost doubled in size (don't worry, they will have flattened a little), score them deeply down the middle of the length of each loaf with a lame or thin razorblade. Turn the oven down to 220°C and bake the loaves for 20 minutes. Reduce the heat to 180°C and bake for another 15–20 minutes. When the loaves are ready, they should sound very resonant and hollow if you knock on their crusty bases. Cool on a wire cooling rack until at least tepid before cutting. Eat with lots of butter and Vegemite.

40-year old bung spatula
we bought when we first
arrived in Australia

THE
BEST ROASTED
SMASHED
POTATOES

I'm not one of those fancy potato people. I've tried all kinds and I find all of them work, with degrees of difference not worth worrying about. I've had the most gorgeous desirees and terrible kipflers so, at the end of the day, I believe it's how they're grown and luck of the draw. The most important piece of information you need is to allow PLENTY of time. Crunch is not a skill but a time investment, so allow at least 2 hours from boiling to the end of roasting. Serve as a beer snack or accompaniment to a myriad of meals. Vegans can replace the butter with olive oil or a veg-based spread such as Nuttelex.

2 kg potatoes (any variety), skins left on (but scrubbed well) or peeled

100–150 g butter, softened

Salt & freshly ground black pepper

A few sprigs of thyme OR rosemary

FEEDS 4–6 AS A SIDE

GF / DFO / V / VGO

Preheat the oven to 200°C fan-forced. Line two large baking trays with baking paper.

Steam or boil the potatoes until tender. If boiling, salt the water to taste.

Dot the potatoes on the baking trays, making sure there is a 1–2 cm space between them so it doesn't get too steamy (you may need to use a third tray). Use a spoon to press down on each potato so it splits as much or as little as you want. The more the taters fall apart, the more jaw-breaking crunchy bits you'll get (which I love but not everyone does). If you like softer centres, try to keep them together (not peeling helps here too). Place about 1 teaspoon of butter on each potato – maybe 2 teaspoons for larger ones – then season well.

Roast the potatoes for about 1½ hours or simply until they are as crunchy as you like, turning them once or twice so they colour evenly. Only add the herbs towards the end for about 1 minute or they'll get incinerated rather than infuse deliciously into the potatoes. Taste and season.

Pohtadude

MY TWO FAVE SALAD DRESSINGS:
DIJON-LEMON & HONEY-BALSAMIC

I used to be asked for the recipes for these dressings endless times each day when I had my cafe at the Adelaide Central Market. They're completely versatile – the dijon–lemon is sharp and clean (great for a green leaf or garden salad), while the honey–balsamic is deeper and sweet (good for more robust salads and things like roasted veg).

DIJON-LEMON DRESSING

3 tablespoons lemon juice (apple cider vinegar or white wine vinegar are also good!)

3 tablespoons olive oil

1 heaped teaspoon dijon mustard

1 garlic clove, crushed (optional)

½ teaspoon sugar

Salt, to taste

HONEY-BALSAMIC DRESSING

3 tablespoons balsamic vinegar

3 tablespoons olive oil

1 heaped teaspoon wholegrain mustard

1 garlic clove, crushed (optional)

1 teaspoon honey

Salt, to taste

EACH DRESSING MAKES
125 ML (½ CUP)

GF / DF / V

Combine all the ingredients for each salad dressing in clean glass jars and shake until emulsified.

If you add the garlic on the day, these dressings can be premade and kept in airtight jars in the fridge for a few weeks.

NOT-BORING ROASTED BROCCOLI & SWEET POTATO

I'd say this is in my top three dinner-for-one picks. I love the purity and complexity of flavour you can get from such simple ingredients when you bother to engage with the details. The trick is high heat for slightly charred edges, to bring out the hint of bitter complexity and nuttiness in the veggies and also to allow enough time for the sugars to develop. If you are missing some 'meatiness', you can finish with a sprinkle of finely shredded nori or roughly chopped roasted almonds when serving.

1 head of broccoli OR cauliflower (or use ½ head of each), cut into 4 cm florets

Olive oil

Salt & freshly ground black pepper

1 large sweet potato, peeled & diced into 2 cm pieces

A few sprigs of rosemary OR thyme

½ lemon

FEEDS 2–3
DF / GF / VG

Preheat the oven to 250°C fan-forced. Line two baking trays with baking paper.

Toss the broccoli and/or cauliflower with enough olive oil to coat the pieces lightly. Season, then spread onto one of the baking trays in a single layer.

Toss the sweet potato with enough olive oil to coat the pieces lightly. Season, then spread onto the second baking tray in a single layer.

Place both trays in the oven. The broccoli or cauliflower will take about 10–15 minutes. It should emerge from the oven with slightly charred edges and a tiny residual bite. The sweet potato will need a little more time. It should emerge tender with charred edges. I like to nestle the rosemary or thyme into the sweet potato when the broccoli comes out of the oven, to catch the residual heat and infuse gently, rather than becoming incinerated and bitter.

To serve, pile everything into bowls and finish with a squeeze of lemon.

CASSIE LEE'S NO-COOK TOMATO SAUCE

This recipe is incredibly special, not only because it's bloody delish and a cinch to make, but also because the kid I babysat from when she was a week-old bubba taught it to me after returning from a life-changing trip to Italy. Only the mystical sorcery of industrious matriarchs would be able to come up with something so perfect from chucking very few and basic ingredients into a blender for mere seconds. All you cruddy cooks out there, this one's got yer name on it!

1 x 250–300 g punnet of cherry tomatoes

3–4 tablespoons olive oil

2 garlic cloves, peeled

Handful of basil leaves

50–80 g (⅓–½ cup) raw almonds

Salt & freshly ground black pepper

FEEDS 4

GF / DF / VG

Place the tomatoes, olive oil, garlic, basil and almonds in a blender and blitz until smooth. Taste and season with salt and pepper. THAT'S IT!

Fold the sauce through the Handmade Semolina Cavatelli (page 135). A nice way to change it up is to mix a batch of the Not-Boring Roasted Broccoli (page 22) into the sauce before adding it to the pasta.

I read somewhere that life's about how you choose to tell your story, not what's actually happened to you. I try to view pear-shaped situations through a lens of 'how can I be responsible for my own healing?' because this is the only thing I can control. I've learnt the hard way that resting in a state of victimhood will always place you at the mercy of others to do the right thing. You cannot alter the past nor the actions of others, only your own framing of situations.

To get intense pigment stains off your hands ...

1.
Use about 1 teaspoon of bicarbonate of soda.

2.
Rub into the stains, then rinse with warm water.

MELTDOWN RAMEN

I call this meltdown ramen because it's the safest thing to attempt when you are feeling delicate and can't handle rejection from fussy eaters, or just flying solo and avoiding an emotional spill. These times require zero brain exertion, but still demand succour and definitely comfort. So I give you not a recipe, but a bunch of cheaty imperatives to have in the fridge or freezer, which can instantly transform a humble packet of 2-minute noods (hit your local Asian grocer for more interesting options) into a meal befitting a pyjamaed queen. Your job is to add whatever makes you happiest.

USE 1 PACKET OF INSTANT NOODS PER PERSON, THEN FREESTYLE AWAY
DF / VGO

B – add at the beginning   M – add mid-cook   E – add at the end

UMAMI

Pre-sliced dried shiitake mushrooms – B

Wakame (dried seaweed) – M

Kimchi – E

PROTEIN OR BULK

Fish, squid OR prawn balls (found in the freezer or fridge section of Asian grocers) – B

Mushrooms – B

Tofu puffs (found in the fridge section of Asian grocers) – B

Soft OR silken tofu – M

Fried egg OR whisked egg stirred into hot broth to create a marble effect – E

TEXTURE

Bean curd skins (found in the fridge section of Asian grocers) – M

Cloud ear fungus (dried black fungus; found at Asian grocers) – M

GREENS

Add any of these at the end for a quick blanch only, so they stay crisp

Bok choy – E

Choy sum – E

Wombok – E

Iceberg OR cos lettuce – E

Bean sprouts – E

Julienned nashi pear – E

HERBAGE & SPRINKLES

Add any of these as garnish after plating

Roughly chopped coriander – E

Sliced spring onion – E

Sliced chilli – E

Fried shallots – E

CREATE A RAMEN RUCKUS WITH ...

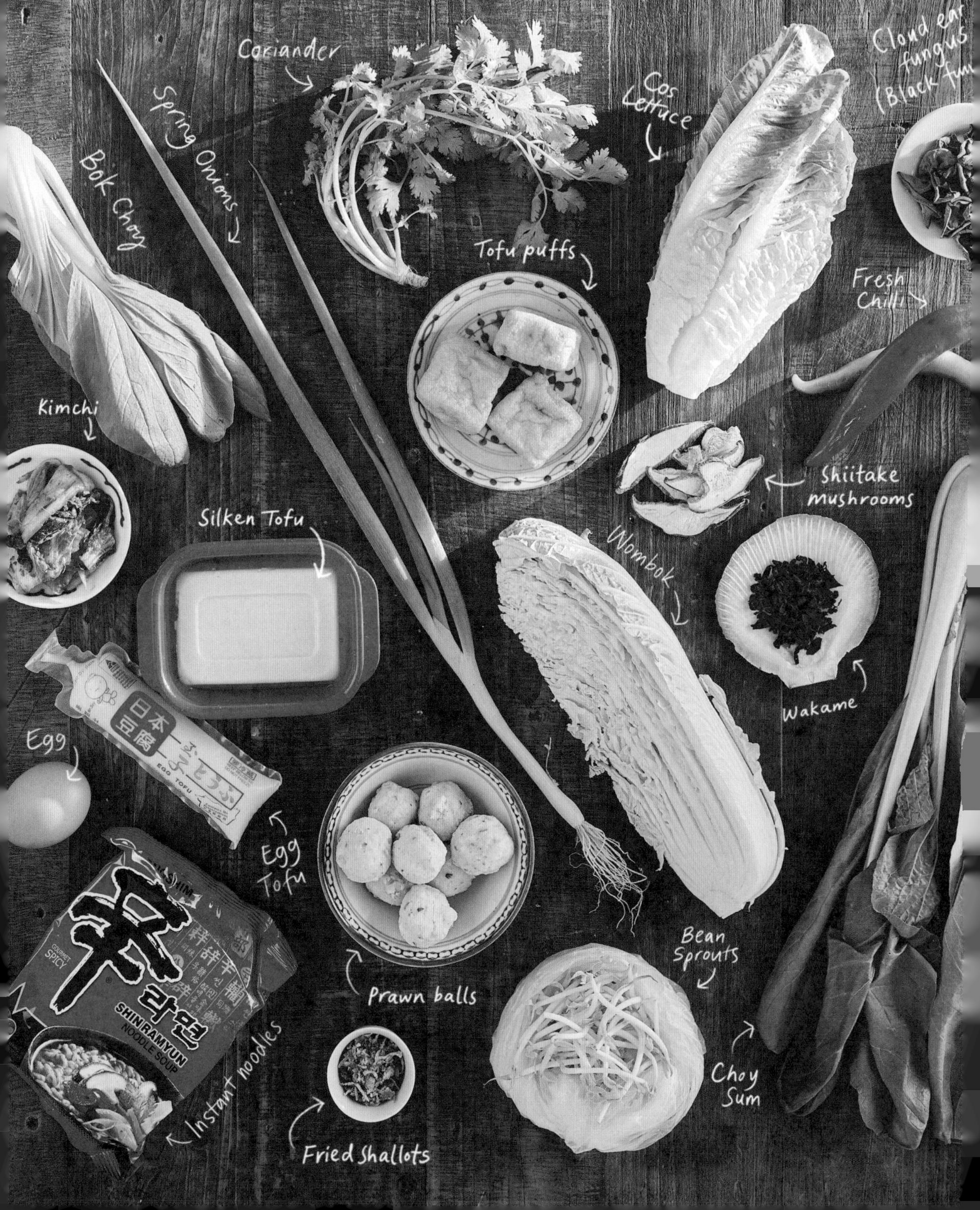

Coriander

Spring Onions

Bok Choy

Cos Lettuce

Cloud ear fungus (Black fun...

Tofu puffs

Fresh Chilli

Kimchi

Shiitake mushrooms

Silken Tofu

Wombok

Wakame

Egg

日本豆腐

Egg Tofu

Bean Sprouts

SHIN RAMYUN NOODLE SOUP

Prawn balls

Choy Sum

Instant noodles

Fried Shallots

SALTY
SNACKISH
feeling peckish?

LIFE-CHANGING
GUACAMOLE

If this isn't the best guacamole you've ever tasted, I'll seriously eat my jocks. What makes it extra tasty is the Tabasco. Scoop the guacamole with corn chips, dollop it in a tortilla or spread a thick layer of it on rustic toast with a couple of poachies on top for a zingy brekky. However you choose to guac, it's a winner!

2 avocados, stones removed, flesh roughly chopped with a spoon, then scooped out of the skin

½ small red onion, finely chopped OR ½ cup finely sliced spring onion

1 x 250–300 g punnet of cherry tomatoes OR 2 vine-ripened tomatoes, diced into 1 cm pieces

½ cup firmly packed roughly chopped coriander, stalks included

1 teaspoon Tabasco sauce, or to taste (you can also use finely chopped pickled jalapeños, to taste)

1 teaspoon caster sugar

½ teaspoon each salt & freshly ground black pepper

Up to 3 tablespoons freshly squeezed lime OR lemon juice

FEEDS 4–6 AS A SNACK

GF / DF / VG

Place all the ingredients, but only HALF the lime or lemon juice, in a medium bowl and gently fold them together. Taste the guacamole, then balance the seasoning with more salt and/or the remaining lime or lemon juice, if needed.

CRISPY NORI CHIPS

Mum came home from a trip to Malaysia with this geniously simple snack, taught to her by one of her aunties. It's a great one for getting the kids to help with, but expect half the batch to go straight down the hatch as it tends to quickly turn into an eat-as-you-go affair!

1 packet of large spring roll wrappers

3 large eggs, whisked

1 packet of nori sheets

2 litres rice bran OR sunflower oil, for deep-frying

SEASONINGS

Icing sugar, to taste

Fine salt, to taste

Shichimi togarashi (Japanese chilli powder; found at Asian grocers), to taste

FEEDS 10 AS A SNACK

DF / V

With a pastry brush, thoroughly paint a spring roll wrapper with egg, then press a sheet of nori firmly on top of the wrapper, making sure the edges are aligned. If there's a bit of excess wrapper around the border, don't sweat it. Repeat until all the spring roll wrappers are used up. Snip into roughly 6 x 4 cm rectangles with scissors.

Heat the oil in a medium saucepan over medium–high heat. To test if the oil is ready, rest the tips of a pair of wooden chopsticks on the base of the pan, and if a steady flurry of bubbles rises to the surface, it's ready. If it's very vigorous, it's likely the oil is too hot. Fry handfuls of the rectangles until they curl up and turn golden and crisp. If they quickly turn dark, turn the heat down a few notches or pour a dash of unheated oil into the pan to cool it down. Scoop the nori chips out with a spider ladle or slotted spoon and drain them in a paper towel–lined colander. Repeat until all the chips are cooked.

For a sweet finish, dust the chips with icing sugar. For a savoury finish, season with salt and the shichimi togarashi. But guess what my fave is? Yup, all three together for sweet, salty, spicy fun times!

These store brilliantly for up to a month in an airtight container, but should be eaten fresh if you've added the sugar.

Chopping nuts or herbs?
Use two knives in tandem and the
job gets done in half the time.

'I'm often asked about the close relationships I have with my exes and how I do it. It certainly helps that there were no kids. If you have enough curiosity and stamina to go through the rubble of a mangled marriage, discard the non-working parts and find the skerricks of what fundamentally drew you together at the beginning, something miraculous happens – the friendship regrows as unbreakable. It's unorthodox and perhaps people are disappointed when I say there's no juicy drama behind the scenes, but there really isn't. In fact, we all get along better now without the angst of having to make things work. There's release and reinvention in relationships if you can agree to disagree and acknowledge everyone's emotional truths ARE truths!'

BRAZILIAN CHEESE BREAD (PÃO DE QUEIJO)

I first tried this moreish little number at my friends' Leo and Myke's home for a lovely rainy night supper and became immediately obsessed. Myke is Brazilian and this is a favourite snack from his home country. Think delicious cheesy-flavoured profiteroles but with a mochi-like texture and you have Brazilian cheese bread. And the brilliant thing is they take no time to whizz up – a perfect from-scratch after-school snack!

Olive oil spray

1 large egg

80 ml (⅓ cup) olive oil

160 ml (⅔ cup) milk

195 g (1½ cups) tapioca flour*

50 g (½ cup) finely grated parmesan OR any kind of cheese you like

1 teaspoon salt

MAKES ABOUT 30

GF / V

Preheat the oven to 200°C fan-forced. Grease three 12-hole mini muffin tins with olive oil spray.

Blitz all the ingredients in a blender until smooth, then fill the muffin-tin holes about three-quarters of the way up the sides. If you only have one mini muffin tin, and are baking in two batches, make sure you stir the mixture well before loading up the tin again as tapioca flour settles. Bake for about 15 minutes or until pale golden.

These are best eaten fresh on the day or can be cooled and frozen in ziplock bags, then easily reheated in the oven for snack attacks – cook from frozen at 190°C fan-forced for about 20 minutes, until warmed through.

*I find Asian brands work best.

KIMCHI, FRIED SEAWEED, RICE

By far my fave savoury midnight snack, and very good with a beer. This isn't so much a recipe as it is introducing a way of eating. Koshihikari rice is a Japanese variety of short-grain rice known for its robust bite and high starch content, which gives it a lovely sticky quality. Of course, you can use any variety of rice that's leftover in the fridge, but koshihikari is the most satisfying for this combination.

Kimchi

Cooked koshihikari rice (found at most supermarkets) OR medium-grain white rice

Korean fried seaweed sheets (found at Asian grocers)

FEEDS 1

GF / DF / VGO (USE VEGAN KIMCHI)

Simply pop a couple of pieces of kimchi on the rice, then, on top of this place a piece or two of the seaweed. Using your chopsticks, press downwards on the outer edges of the seaweed so it scoops and wraps around a mouthful of rice and the kimchi together to make a rough parcel. If you're confused by my instructions, just pop a bit of each on a spoon and go for it!

SPAM OMELETTE SANDWICHES

This was as close to normal sandwiches as I ever got in my school lunchbox – made by my beloved Great Aunty Kim, so they'll forever remind me of her. And it's for this very reason that I cannot and will not unlike Spam. Growing up in the tropics with no tradition of cold meats, meat in a tin it was. It's embedded in my palate memory as totally delicious and there's nothing I can do about it. Don't pooh-pooh until you try it, all you judgey wudgeys!

170 g (½ tin) Spam, diced into 5 mm pieces

2 teaspoons vegetable oil

4 eggs, lightly whisked

Butter, for spreading

8 slices of white bread

8 leaves of iceberg lettuce OR 1 continental cucumber, finely sliced

Salt & freshly ground black pepper

Ketchup (optional)

FEEDS 4

In a large non-stick frying pan over medium heat, stir-fry the Spam in the oil until the edges are golden. Add the egg and fry until the omelette is half cooked through, then flip it over and cook until the omelette is cooked through and golden on both sides. Don't stress if the flipping unleashes a bit of cosmetic chaos – it's fun dining not fine dining we're talking about here! Divide the omelette into four serves and cool before using.

To assemble your sandwiches, butter the bread, then add some omelette, a double layer of iceberg lettuce or a layer of sliced cucumber, then season with salt and pepper. I'm thinking a little squiggle of ketchup on one side of the bread wouldn't go astray either!

SESAME-PICKLED CUCUMBERS

These cucumber pickles are insanely moreish. They are brilliant as a snack but also go wonderfully with my Korean-Style 5–Minute Spicy Chicken on page 88. Crunchy, nutty, salty, sour, sweet, spicy and garlicky all at once … I'm salivating just writing this.

3–4 large continental cucumbers, unpeeled

1 teaspoon salt

PICKLING LIQUID

180 ml (¾ cup) light soy sauce OR tamari

250 ml (1 cup) white vinegar

110 g (½ cup) sugar

3 tablespoons sesame oil

1–2 red bird's eye chillies, sliced

1 head of garlic, cloves separated, peeled & bashed to just split

MAKES ABOUT 2 x 500 ML JARS
GFO / DF / VG

Cut the cucumbers into quarters lengthways and slice the seeds away. Slice them diagonally into 4–5 mm thick spears.

Toss the cucumber in a colander with the salt and refrigerate uncovered for 1 hour with a plate underneath to catch the liquid.

Meanwhile, to make the pickling liquid, stir all the ingredients in a large bowl until well combined and most of the sugar has dissolved.

Squeeze the heck out of the cucumber in handfuls, to remove all excess liquid, then combine with the pickling liquid. Stir well and refrigerate overnight in an airtight container before eating.

These pickles will keep well refrigerated for up to 3 weeks.

TOMATO, BURRATA, ANCHOVIES & BALSAMIC

It's always the simplest things that strike me most when I travel. I had a version of this dish in Bologna in a busy strip of eateries and it was a revelation in quality. If you can track down home-grown tomatoes and buy the best burrata, anchovies and balsamic you can afford, you will taste a profound difference. You can drape the tomatoes with thin slices of Italian prosciutto if you're not a fan of anchovies, or omit both to make this vegetarian.

3–4 tomatoes, sliced 7 mm thick

Sea salt flakes & freshly ground
black pepper

1 ball of burrata

A few very thin slices of onion (doesn't
matter what kind), rings separated

Handful of basil leaves, torn

1–2 tins Ortiz anchovies (yes, I can
easily down a tin on my own!) OR
10 thin slices of Italian prosciutto

A few drizzles of aged balsamic vinegar

A few glugs of olive oil

FEEDS 3–4 AS A STARTER

GF / VO

Cover a dinner plate with the tomatoes, then season methodically with salt and pepper.

Place the burrata in the middle, scatter the onion and basil on top, then drape the anchovies or prosciutto evenly over the surface. Drizzle the balsamic over everything (not too much), then finish with a generous amount of olive oil.

Always zest citrus before eating and freeze it in the zest bank for adding a pop of flavour to things like creams, custards, pastries, salad dressings, marinades and pasta sauces.

'I always allow myself time to pause and notice the small things. Never let yourself get so busy and jaded that you miss the beauty that exists every day and everywhere. I once took a video of a caterpillar as it moved across my patio at surprising breakneck speed in a dead straight line, then paused to make a left turn. I re-watch it quite regularly to remind myself that I'm part of something beyond understanding. Watching this thing with a tiny brain make a decision. Whether it was 'I'm hungry and I smell green to my left' or 'Holy shizenhousen my biological clock is tickin' and I gotta get me a branch to weave a cocoon against real quick!' is a delightful mystery! It's one of the reasons why I love having a garden so much. Blink and the trees are suddenly naked, green, a memory. Next, spring buds surging with life force have pushed their tiny heads through dormant wood. And before you know it, the blossoms have exploded. Forget to look up and breathe, and they've shed without warning like pink snowfall, replaced by the beginnings of green. To be reminded of the impermanence of beauty and the beauty of impermanence are wonderfully sobering daily thoughts.'

MARIA'S CHARGRILLED VEG & PESTO ON FRESH LEPINJI

It would be easy to glance at this recipe and think it nothing unusual, but unless you've honoured the act of chargrilling every piece of vegetable to perfection (with just the right amount of smokiness and crunch), seasoned the pesto with undivided attention, then selected the freshest of bread rolls to sandwich it all in, you won't understand what I'm banging on about here. I first had this when I was still doing make-up and it was a wedding-morning snack at an Italian bride's parents' home. It's haunted me ever since – truly a formative food moment steeped in that signature Italian simplicity, which will never cease to fascinate me. I asked the bride for the pesto recipe and we've been friends ever since. For vegans, substitute the parmesan with a tablespoon of shiro (white) miso, or to taste, and omit the salt.

1 large or 2 small red capsicums

Salt & freshly ground black pepper

Olive oil

2 medium zucchini, cut lengthways into 5 mm thick slices

1 eggplant, cut lengthways into 5 mm thick slices

4 lepinji OR ciabatta rolls (any rustic-style bread roll you want, really, but make sure it's FRESHHH)

PESTO

2 handfuls of basil leaves (if you can find home-grown it makes a world of difference)

180 ml (⅔ cup) olive oil

100 g (1 cup) grated parmesan OR pecorino

Handful of pine nuts OR raw almonds (cheaper!)

2 garlic cloves, peeled

Salt & freshly ground black pepper

FEEDS 4

V / VGO

Preheat the oven to 200°C fan-forced on the grill setting. Line a baking tray with foil and lightly oil it.

Remove the capsicum stem, then cut a slit down one side. Splay the capsicum out, bending any turned-under parts out, then squash it with the palm of your hand so the whole capsicum sits as flat as possible. Place it on the prepared tray, skin-side up, and grill on the highest rack in the oven until the entire surface is blistered black. As soon as it comes out of the oven, scrunch the foil up around the capsicum to seal, and allow to steam and cool (about 10 minutes), then peel all the skin off and discard. Season lightly and cut into four even pieces.

Heat a cast-iron chargrill pan until smoking. Drizzle in a little olive oil, then char the zucchini slices very briefly on both sides until they are slightly wilted and cooked enough for char marks to appear but with a residual crunch. Season very lightly before transferring to a plate lined with a double layer of paper towel. Oil the pan more generously for the eggplant. Season the eggplant slices on both sides, then cook until just tender with good char marks.

To make the pesto, place the basil, olive oil, parmesan or pecorino, pine nuts or almonds, garlic and a modest amount of salt and pepper in a food processor and blitz until well combined. Taste and season further or add more of any of the pesto ingredients if needed.

To assemble, slice the rolls in half, slather with a good amount of pesto on both sides, then layer with the charred vegetables and sandwich together.

The veg can be kept for up to a week refrigerated in an airtight container. The pesto will keep in a jar for 2 days max before losing vitality, but this can be delayed if you flood the surface with 2 mm of olive oil.

SOURDOUGH FRUIT LOAF, PROSCIUTTO, HONEY & CHEESE

My friend Gheeta got me onto this when we were working at the Adelaide Central Market together and we'd hustle bits and pieces from other market vendors at dinnertime. It might seem an unusual combo (although honey and cheese is a very Italian thing) but, trust me, the complex salty and sweet notes of the listed suspects work together like a dream. A few peppery leaves of rocket would go well if your palate yearns for a bit of green.

2–3 very thin slices of Italian prosciutto

Enough sliced raclette OR tilsit cheese (found in specialty shops, but if not, any hard cheese will do) to cover the bread

A zig-zag drizzle of honey

2 slices of very fresh thickly cut sourdough fruit loaf

FEEDS 1

Assemble the ingredients in the order listed between the two slices of bread.

SALTY

BOWL FOOD

food that hugs

AVGOLEMONO

Think clean, comforting chicken soup, but with rice and lemon, and you have Greek avgolemono – perfect for all the occasions when one turns to traditional chicken soup, except this one has a gorgeous hit of acidity. Honestly, I could eat bowls of this night after night after night.

1 whole chook

2 onions, finely diced

2 carrots, peeled & diced into 1 cm pieces

2 celery stalks, diced into 1 cm pieces

1 teaspoon salt

½ cup roughly chopped flat-leaf parsley leaves, plus extra to serve

4 eggs

180 ml (¾ cup) lemon juice

1 cup cooked white OR brown rice

Salt & freshly ground black pepper

FEEDS 6

GF / DF

Cover the chook with water in a large saucepan and simmer, uncovered, until the flesh is cooked through. Remove the chicken from the broth and, when cool enough, shred all the flesh with your fingers. Discard the bones.

Add the onion, carrot, celery and salt to the broth. Simmer for about 15 minutes, then add the shredded chicken and parsley. Return to a simmer and cook for another 10–15 minutes.

Whisk the eggs and lemon juice in a medium bowl, then whisk in a ladle of the hot broth to temper the egg mixture a little – this helps prevent it from curdling when it hits the soup. Whisk this mixture briskly into the simmering soup. You want it to turn milky but not curdle*, so allow it to slowly come back to a simmer, but don't boil. Remove from the heat, add the rice, then taste and season with salt and pepper. Garnish with extra parsley and serve.

This will keep for up to a week refrigerated in an airtight container and for up to a month in the freezer.

*If it does curdle, don't sweat it. The texture might not be ideal, but the flavour will reign supreme!

SESAME OMELETTE SOUP WITH RICE VERMICELLI

This is the kind of thing I love going home to Mum's to eat – a bowl of unassuming, calming noods, which usually turns into three bowls ... not carb-phobic. For vegos, omit the pork, double the shiitake mushroom quantity and use veg instead of chicken stock.

3 tablespoons sesame oil

2 large eggs, lightly whisked

2 garlic cloves, crushed

200 g pork fillet, cut into batons

5–6 dried shiitake mushrooms (soaked in freshly boiled water for 30 minutes, drained & quartered if large)

1.2 litres chicken stock

100 g thin rice vermicelli noodles, soaked in cold water for 10–15 minutes & drained

2 teaspoons light soy sauce OR tamari

Salt & white pepper

2 heads of bok choy OR choy sum, cut into 5 cm pieces

FEEDS 2

GFO / DF / VO

In a non-stick frying pan, heat HALF the sesame oil over medium–high heat, add the egg and cook the omelette until nicely browned. While it's cooking, use a spatula to chop the omelette into bite-sized pieces. Remove from the heat and set aside.

Combine the remaining sesame oil and the garlic in a medium saucepan and sauté until it just begins to turn a pale golden colour. Add the pork and mushrooms and cook for about 2 minutes, until the pork is cooked through. Add the chicken stock and omelette and bring to the boil. Lower the heat and simmer for about 5 minutes.

Just before serving, add the vermicelli and soy sauce. Agitate with chopsticks to heat through. Taste to check the noodles are tender, then season further with salt and white pepper. Place the bok choy or choy sum at the bottom of the serving bowls, then ladle the noodles and soup over the top. Serve immediately.

MAPO TOFU

This is one of the most moreish dishes you will ever have with rice. It's the classic push–pull Szechuanese heat that makes you sweat, tingle and feel numb but still want to go back for more. For vegos and vegans, sub out the mince for 10 large dried shiitake mushrooms, rehydrated in boiling water for 30 minutes, then drained and diced into 5 mm pieces, and use veg instead of chicken stock.

125 ml (½ cup) vegetable oil

1 tablespoon dried chilli flakes

1 tablespoon ground Szechuan peppercorns

3 tablespoons finely shredded ginger

3 garlic cloves, finely chopped

200 g pork, chicken OR beef mince

2 bird's eye chillies, split lengthways down the middle

2 tablespoons doubanjiang (fermented chilli bean paste; found in the Asian section of supermarkets or at Asian grocers)

80 g Chinese pickled mustard heart (found at Asian grocers), cut into matchsticks (optional)

2 tablespoons Shaoxing rice wine

170 ml chicken stock

¼ teaspoon sesame oil

¼ teaspoon sugar

1½ teaspoons wheaten cornflour, mixed with 2 tablespoons water just before needed

500 g silken tofu, diced into 2 cm pieces

Light soy sauce, to taste

2 spring onions, finely sliced

Handful of coriander leaves, roughly chopped

Steamed rice OR Chinese steamed buns (found in the freezer section of Asian grocers), to serve

FEEDS 2

DF / VGO

To make the chilli oil, combine HALF the vegetable oil, the chilli flakes and Szechuan pepper in a small saucepan over medium heat and stir until nutty and fragrant. Remove from the heat and set aside.

In a medium non-stick frying pan, combine the remaining vegetable oil, the ginger and garlic and sauté until a pale golden colour. Add your minced meat of choice and the chillies, increase the heat to high, then stir-fry until cooked through.

Stir in the doubanjiang and pickled mustard heart (if using), then add the Shaoxing rice wine, chicken stock, sesame oil and sugar. Allow the sauce to come to a simmer before briskly stirring in the cornflour slurry. When the sauce has thickened, add the tofu, then strain the prepared chilli oil through a sieve directly over the tofu. Fold to combine all the ingredients, then taste for seasoning. Add some light soy sauce if needed.

Garnish with the spring onion and coriander and serve with steamed rice or Chinese steamed buns.

It's important for me to do my own dirty work. For my creatively manic personality type, housework is the litmus. If I can't enjoy looking after myself, my fur sons and home, it's a clear sign of work–life imbalance. It makes me feel disconnected and anxious. We live in an age where we seem to subcontract everything, even our emotions and grief, because there's so much pressure to be successful in our careers. Stuff like grieving is normal and important. Don't cheat yourself out of the resilience and wisdom gained if you are able to muster up the courage and time to work through it.

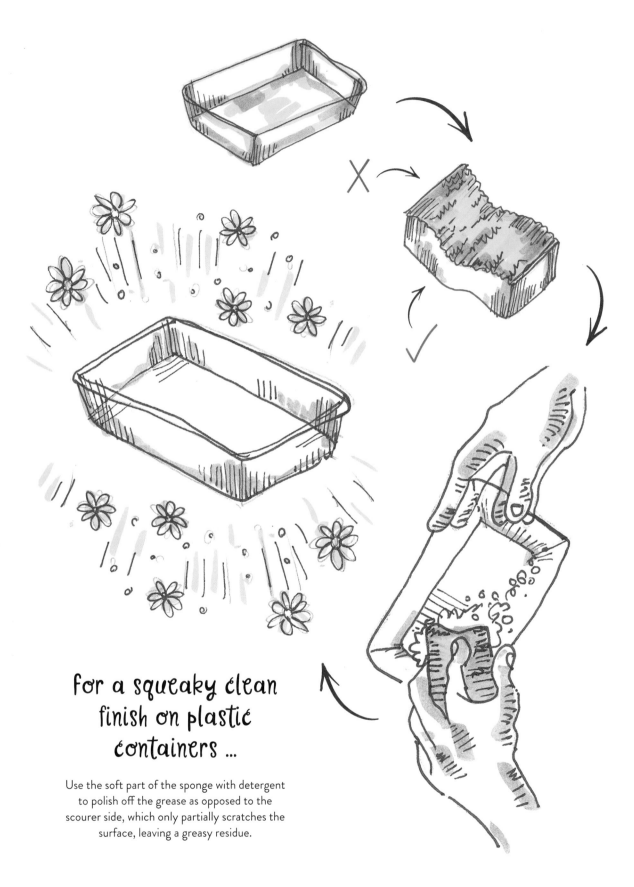

for a squeaky clean finish on plastic containers ...

Use the soft part of the sponge with detergent to polish off the grease as opposed to the scourer side, which only partially scratches the surface, leaving a greasy residue.

COCONUT CHICKEN CONGEE WITH LIME

The idea for this zingy bowl of yum first happened when I was craving the comfort of a basic chicken congee but, out of sheer laziness and wish for speed, tipped in a container of leftover coconut rice from a nasi lemak that my mum had dropped off to me the night before. Think chicken congee with a bit more tropical bang for your buck.

2 tablespoons olive oil

2 garlic cloves, crushed

2 cm piece of ginger, finely chopped

3 spring onions, finely sliced, plus extra to serve

2 long red chillies, finely sliced, plus extra to serve

2 tablespoons Shaoxing rice wine

200 g (1 cup) jasmine rice

2 litres chicken stock

250 ml (1 cup) coconut milk

2 chicken breast fillets OR 4–5 thigh fillets

3 tablespoons lime juice

Fish sauce, to taste

1 cup roughly chopped coriander, including stalks

35 g (½ cup) fried shallots

FEEDS 4–5

GF / DF

Combine the olive oil, garlic, ginger, spring onion and chilli in a large non-stick saucepan over medium–high heat and sauté until golden and fragrant. Add the Shaoxing rice wine, rice, stock, coconut milk and chicken. Bring to the boil, then simmer with the lid slightly ajar until the chicken is just cooked through and the rice is broken down to a soupy consistency – the chicken will cook quicker so keep your eye on it.

Remove the chicken and shred with clean hands or two forks, then return it to the pan. Stir in the lime juice and fish sauce. If the congee is a little gluggy, simply add water until it reaches the consistency you like, but do taste and season again.

Serve hot with extra spring onion, chilli, coriander leaves and a sprinkle of fried shallots.

FAST PHO

A traditional pho can take an entire day to make, but this version takes a mere 35 minutes in a pressure cooker and honestly packs as much flavour as one that's been simmering for hours. I opt for pull-apart beef rather than the traditional finely sliced kind, because it's what's used to make the stock, so it's the obvious thing to do. Don't fret if you don't have a pressure cooker – it will be about a 2-hour old-fashioned simmer on the stove with an equally brilliant result.

6 garlic cloves, peeled

50 g ginger, peeled

6 cloves

4 star anise

1 cinnamon stick

3 teaspoons black peppercorns

1.5–2 kg brisket, larger chunks of fat cut away & reserved, sliced into 2–3 cm steaks

2 small–medium brown onions, each peeled & roughly cut into 6 chunks

2 litres water

125 ml (½ cup) fish sauce

2 tablespoons caster sugar

1 kg fresh flat rice noodles

½ small white OR brown onion, finely sliced

BITS & PIECES

125 ml (½ cup) hoisin sauce

80 ml (⅓ cup) sriracha chilli sauce

300 g (3⅓ cups) bean sprouts

14 sprigs of Thai basil

⅓ cup sliced long red chilli OR bird's eye chilli

Lemon wedges

FEEDS UP TO 7

GFO (USE GF HOISIN) / DF

With a mortar and pestle, lightly bash the garlic, ginger and all the spices separately, so they are just broken but no more.

Melt the reserved fat from the brisket in a large saucepan or pressure cooker over medium–low heat, until you have about 2 tablespoons of liquid (or use 2 tablespoons of vegetable oil). Discard the solid fat then add the garlic, ginger, spices and chunks of onion. Sauté over medium–high heat for 4 minutes until very fragrant, then stir in the water, fish sauce and sugar. Add the beef, secure the cover and pressure-cook for 35 minutes – or, if you are using a regular saucepan, place on the lowest simmer and cook, covered, for 2 hours or until the beef easily pulls apart.

Remove the beef from the broth and shred with two forks, removing any excess fat. Strain the broth through a sieve to remove the aromatics and spices. If there is a lot of fat on the surface, skim off and discard. Return the broth and shredded beef to the pressure cooker or saucepan, add the noodles and sliced onion, cover, then wait for 5 minutes for the noodles to soften.

Serve piping hot with the bits and pieces in the centre of the table. The hoisin and sriracha are for dipping the beef in, so place these in individual dishes.

Oops, forgot zee onion!

EASY SWEET SOY PORK WITH OYSTER CONGEE & SPICY PICKLED RADISHES

I had to publish this recipe because it's what I would have served up had I made it to the final of *MasterChef: Back To Win* (Season 12) – a Chinese version of surf and turf! The sweet soy pork gets South Asians all nostalgic because so many versions of it exist across the region, always affiliated with home cooking and the nurture of old matriarchs. Pair it with Teochew-style briny congee* and spicy pickled radish and, dare I say, it's a bloody good dish. Heads up on the radishes – they need to be made a day ahead.

*Teochew-style congee is my favourite. It's cooked until the rice just starts to break down so the texture is more watery and the grains separate, rather than the more well-known, gruelly kind.

SPICY PICKLED RADISH

375 ml (1½ cups) white OR rice wine vinegar

250 g sugar

1 bird's eye chilli, split in half lengthways

30 radishes, topped & tailed, then quartered

1 teaspoon salt

1 tablespoon Laoganma brand crispy chilli oil (found in the Asian section of supermarkets or at Asian grocers)

SWEET SOY PORK

70 g ginger, peeled if old, skin left on if new

3 garlic cloves, peeled

2 tablespoons vegetable oil

3 spring onions, finely sliced

1 kg pork belly, cut into 3 cm pillars

2 teaspoons red fermented rice**, pounded to a fine powder with a mortar & pestle (optional)

750 ml (3 cups) water

1 cinnamon stick

2 star anise

3 cloves

1 large strip of orange peel

70 g (⅓ cup) raw sugar

2 tablespoons Shaoxing rice wine

3½ tablespoons light soy sauce OR tamari

2 tablespoons dark soy sauce OR tamari

OYSTER CONGEE

150 g (¾ cup) jasmine OR long-grain white rice, soaked for 30 minutes in cool water, drained

2 cm piece of ginger, finely sliced

1 litre (4 cups) water

250 g fresh oyster flesh, chopped

TO SERVE

½ cup roughly chopped coriander OR Chinese celery leaves

30 g (½ cup) finely sliced spring onion

White pepper

3 tablespoons light soy sauce OR tamari, if needed

FEEDS 6

GFO / DF

To make the spicy pickled radish, mix the vinegar, sugar and chilli in a bowl. Toss the radish with the salt in a colander and rest, uncovered, in the fridge overnight or for a minimum of 3–4 hours, with a plate underneath to catch any liquid. Combine the radish and pickling liquid in a clean glass jar and allow to pickle overnight. When ready to use, drain the liquid away and toss with the crispy chilli oil. If not drained, the pickled radish will keep well refrigerated for about 2 weeks.

To make the sweet soy pork, pound the ginger and garlic with a mortar and pestle until the ingredients just split.

Combine the vegetable oil, pounded ginger and garlic and the spring onion in a large heavy-based saucepan and sauté over high heat until fragrant and golden. Add the pork, red fermented rice powder (if using), water, cinnamon stick, star anise, cloves and orange peel. Bring to the boil, then reduce to a simmer and add the sugar, Shaoxing rice wine and light and dark soy sauces. Stir to combine and cook, covered, for 1 hour, then reduce to an even lower simmer and cook, uncovered, for another 30–40 minutes, or until the pork is so tender that the lean portion of the meat breaks apart easily when pressed with a fork.

To make the oyster congee, combine the rice, ginger and water in a saucepan and bring to the boil. Simmer until the rice is just starting to break down, then turn the heat off and stir in the chopped oysters.

Divide the congee among bowls and top with the coriander or Chinese celery, spring onion and white pepper to taste. Serve with the pork and pickled radish. If more seasoning is needed in the congee, add some light soy sauce or tamari.

**Red fermented rice is found at Asian grocers but can be omitted or replaced with a dash of red food colouring.

COMFORTING KALE, COCONUT & BEETROOT CURRY

This is one of my favourite anti-waste recipes or what I call 'binner'. It's got kick-arse amounts of depth and flavour for something you can whip up in so little time, but it's also incredibly versatile. So long as you follow the base recipe, once you get to the beetroot and kale you can swap them out for just about any vegetable – cauli and potato, sweet potato and spinach, pea and pumpkin – the perfect candidates are things that look a little bit sad in the vegetable drawer.

2–3 tablespoons olive oil, butter OR ghee

1 large onion, finely diced

1 tablespoon ground turmeric

3 teaspoons ground cumin

1–2 teaspoons dried chilli flakes OR 1 fresh green OR red chilli, chopped

10 sprigs of curry leaves

1 tablespoon grated ginger (or peeled & pounded to a pulp with a mortar & pestle)

3 large beetroot (about 540 g in total), peeled, quartered & sliced 5 mm–1 cm thick

300 g kale leaves, stripped from stem

250 g (1 cup) split red lentils

250 ml (1 cup) coconut milk

1 litre (4 cups) vegetable stock

1 teaspoon salt, or to taste

TO SERVE

Steamed basmati OR brown rice (2 cups uncooked rice should feed 6)

1 bunch of coriander, roughly chopped, including stalks

35 g (½ cup) fried shallots

260 g (1 cup) Greek yoghurt (optional)

FEEDS UP TO 6

GF / DFO / V / VGO

Combine the olive oil, onion, turmeric, cumin, chilli and curry leaves in a large saucepan over medium–high heat. Sauté until the onion is brown and the spices are very fragrant. Add the ginger and sauté for 30 seconds, then stir in the beetroot, kale, lentils, coconut milk, stock and salt. Bring to the boil, then reduce to a simmer and cook, partially covered, until the beetroot is tender.

Serve the curry on a bed of steamed rice, topped with coriander, a sprinkle of fried shallots and a generous dollop of yoghurt.

The curry will keep for up to a week refrigerated in an airtight container.

1.
Dissolve 1 teaspoon of salt in 180 ml (¾ cup) of hot water and add a 10 x 10 cm piece of foil.

To polish silver without a skerrick of elbow grease ...

3.
No polishing required for a sparkling result. PS. Works magnificently for silverware but you'll need larger amounts of solution and bigger bits of foil. Don't stress about being too precise with the recipe – it's not an exact science.

2.
Submerge your tarnished silver jewellery, making sure it touches the foil, and you will witness the most bizarre and satisfying transformation.

'Instead of investing in an expensive dust buster. hit your Asian grocer and grab an old-fashioned straw broom. It's sooooo light and the flexy-as-heck straw fibres manoeuvre like a dream into the narrowest of nooks. This li'l lady's had a bit of duct-tape surgery over the years!'

SALTY

PROPER QUICKIES

Under 15 minutes

Channelling
flavor flav

STEAMED GINGER CHICKEN WITH LAPCHEONG & SHIITAKE MUSHROOMS

Okay self-confessed non-cooks, this is as basic as things gets – cut very few things, mix with sauce, then steam. You'll be high-fiving yourself with the result – wholesome, home-cooked, classic Chinese tastiness. Just gimme a mountain of rice already.

6 chicken thigh fillets, cut into bite-sized pieces

4 lapcheong (Chinese sausage; found at some supermarkets or at Asian grocers), finely sliced

3 tablespoons finely shredded ginger

35 g (1 cup) dried shiitake mushrooms, soaked in freshly boiled water for 30 minutes, drained & finely sliced

2 bunches of gai lan (Chinese broccoli) OR broccolini, cut into 5 cm pieces

4 spring onions, finely sliced

Steamed rice, to serve

SEASONINGS

2 tablespoons wheaten OR maize cornflour

2 tablespoons oyster sauce

1½ tablespoons light soy sauce OR tamari

2 tablespoons Shaoxing rice wine

Pinch of white pepper

2 teaspoons sugar

FEEDS 4

GFO / DF

Mix all the seasonings in a large bowl. Add the chicken, lapcheong, ginger and shiitake mushroom and toss to coat well.

Transfer to a heatproof dish that fits comfortably in a wide saucepan or wok with a lid. Sit the dish on a trivet in the pan, then fill with enough water to just touch the trivet. Cover and steam on a steady simmer for about 12 minutes or until the chicken is cooked through. Nestle the gai lan or broccolini in the mixture and steam briefly, so it remains crunchy but not raw.

Garnish with the spring onion and serve with steamed rice.

TIP

If you want beautiful Chinese restaurant–style curly spring onion for garnishing, slice the spring onions as finely as possible on a steep diagonal and soak in chilled water for a few hours. The longer the soak, the curlier the result.

TAMARIND PRAWNS

I love this classic South-East Asian combination because it's incredibly quick and simple yet produces such a dynamic balance of flavour. You can do a more classic sweet and sour version by substituting the tamarind with ketchup – YUP, ketchup – and if you're not a fan of seafood simply substitute the prawns for finely sliced chicken or pork.

3 tablespoons olive oil

1 red onion, halved & sliced into 5 mm strips lengthways

2–3 garlic cloves, crushed

1 yellow capsicum, quartered lengthways & sliced into 5 mm strips

450 g raw prawns, peeled, deveined & butterflied

80 ml (⅓ cup) tamarind paste OR 3 tablespoons ketchup

2 tablespoons sriracha chilli sauce, or to taste

2 tablespoons sugar

1–2 tablespoons fish sauce, or to taste

TO SERVE

½ cup roughly chopped coriander, including stalks

Steamed rice

FEEDS 3–4 AS A SHARED DISH

GF / DF

Combine the olive oil, onion and garlic in a large non-stick frying pan over high heat. Once it starts to sizzle, cook briefly until the garlic is just starting to turn golden. Add the remaining ingredients and stir-fry until the prawns are just cooked through.

Immediately transfer to a plate, top with the coriander and serve hot with steamed rice.

Fake

Fake

Real

The trick to keeping a bevy of houseplants
looking lush is to do half real, half fake!

When packing clothes into a bag or suitcase ...

Lie everything as flat as possible and you'll be able to fit another one-third of its usual capacity than if you fold or roll.

KOREAN-STYLE 5-MINUTE
SPICY CHICKEN WITH
SESAME-PICKLED CUKES

This dish is SO quick, easy and stupidly delicious. Don't worry when the chicken looks a bit steamy halfway through cooking. When it's done it will be beautifully glossy and saucy. If you don't want to do the pickles, you can eat it with store-bought kimchi or blanched Asian greens, but the cucumber is beautifully refreshing.

1½ tablespoons gochujang (Korean chilli paste; found in the Asian section of supermarkets or at Asian grocers)

1 teaspoon gochugaru (Korean chilli powder; found at Asian grocers) OR chilli powder

2 tablespoons light soy sauce OR tamari

1 tablespoon sesame oil

1 teaspoon sugar

3 tablespoons olive oil

2 large leeks, pale part only, well rinsed of grit & finely sliced OR 6 spring onions, finely sliced

Pinch of salt

1 tablespoon grated ginger (or peeled & pounded to a pulp with a mortar & pestle)

3 garlic cloves, finely chopped or crushed

400–500 g chicken thigh fillets, cut into bite-sized pieces

TO SERVE

Steamed medium-grain rice

Coriander sprigs

Sesame-Pickled Cucumbers (page 46)

FEEDS 4

GFO / DF

Combine the gochujang, gochugaru, soy sauce or tamari, sesame oil and sugar in a small bowl and mix well.

Combine the olive oil, leek or spring onion, salt, ginger and garlic in a medium–large non-stick frying pan over high heat and cook until everything starts to turn a tad golden. Add the chicken and sauce. Stir-fry until the chicken is cooked through and the sauce thickens but stays nice and glossy. AND THAT'S IT!

Serve with steamed rice, coriander and yummo pickled cukes.

TIP

To remove grit from leeks, partially slice them into quarters lengthways (about one-third in from the top), then soak top-side down in a jug of water.

PROPER QUICKIES
88

CHICKEN, LONG BEAN & PRESERVED OLIVE STIR-FRY

This is a stir-fry that just about every Chinese household makes when they have nothing in the fridge AND are not in the mood to think beyond a two-ingredient shop. It's a great example of using meat economically, to add depth of flavour, rather than as the main part of the dish. Mince also cooks very quickly, which is a plus. Just make sure you brown it well before adding the other ingredients 'cause boiled mince is not cool. For anyone who eats mainly veg and is a little anxious about meat prep, mince is your guy.

2 tablespoons olive oil

3 garlic cloves, crushed

1 red chilli (long OR bird's eye), finely sliced

100–200 g coarse chicken mince (with a bit of fat is better for texture & flavour)

2 tablespoons Chinese preserved shredded olive (found at Asian grocers), or to taste

200 g long stringless beans, cut into 1 cm pieces

1 tablespoon Shaoxing rice wine

Pinch of sugar

Dash of oyster sauce, to taste (optional)

Steamed rice, to serve

FEEDS 4

GF / DF

Combine the olive oil, garlic, chilli and chicken mince in a medium non-stick frying pan or wok, then turn the heat to high. When everything starts to sizzle, stir-fry until fragrant and golden. Use a spatula to keep chopping up the mince so it doesn't clump together.

Add the preserved olive, beans, Shaoxing rice wine and sugar and stir until just combined, about 5 seconds. Remove from the heat, taste and add a little oyster sauce if you like, but be mindful the preserved olive is already salty. Serve immediately with steamed rice.

TIP

For perfect stove-top rice, use 1½ cups of water for 1 cup of rice (for brown rice, increase the water to 2 cups). Bring to the boil in a non-stick saucepan, then reduce to the lowest simmer, cover and cook for 10 minutes (or 15 minutes for brown rice). By now, the surface of the rice should be pitted with large holes and no liquid should be visible. Leave covered for another 15 minutes with the heat turned off. Loosen the grains with a thin rubber spatula before serving.

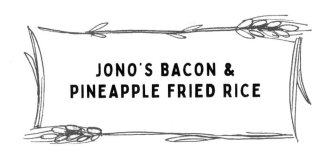

JONO'S BACON & PINEAPPLE FRIED RICE

This recipe fills me with joy and sadness in equal measure. As I get older, I've realised many of life's more meaningful experiences will hold such paradox. It's my favourite dish that Jono used to cook. We're no longer together but remain close friends and there are many happy memories of him spoiling me with this for brekky. It's got that sweet and sour thang going on (to match the emotions), then the bacon and egg which, well, is the most perfect excuse to call it breakfast. I barely drink but it feels like this would make a great hangover cure too!

2 tablespoons olive oil, plus extra

90 g (¾ cup) sliced spring onion

2 sprigs of curry leaves, leaves picked (optional)

½–¾ cup diced bacon OR ham

1 small–medium red capsicum, diced into 1 cm pieces

190 g (1 cup) diced pineapple (bite-sized pieces)

1 cup cooked chilled rice (any variety is fine) OR 1 x 250 g packet of microwave rice (unheated please)

Light soy OR fish sauce, to taste

2 eggs

⅓ cup roughly chopped coriander leaves

Sriracha chilli sauce, to serve

FEEDS 2

GFO / DF

Combine the olive oil, spring onion, curry leaves (if using) and bacon or ham in a large non-stick frying pan over high heat. Stir-fry until fragrant and the edges of the bacon have browned a little. Add the capsicum, pineapple and rice and stir-fry for about 10 seconds until combined or until the rice is tender, then add the soy or fish sauce to taste.

Pour a dash of olive oil into a heavy-based non-stick frying pan over medium heat and fry the eggs to your liking.

To serve, portion the rice into two bowls or plates, then top each with coriander, a fried egg and sriracha to taste.

'I've learnt not to be afraid of making mistakes – it's worse to be paralysed with indecision. 'Poor decisions' can create opportunities to learn about your own nature and catalyse movement. We are taught so often to go for what we want, but it's just as useful to learn (albeit the hard way), what you don't want.'

Freeze portions of pressure/slow-cooked secondary cuts of meat for quick cooks with ready-to-go, melt-in-your-mouth meat.

NO-COOK PUTTANESCA WITH SPAGHETTINI

This is a dangerous one for a carb monster like me, but it makes me SO happy to hoover up a giant bowl of it, especially when I'm on my own. I'm a huge fan of the Jon Banchovies, but here I find them a bit intense. Sometimes, however, I'll add a small can of tuna for a bit more substance and an extra boost of umami. As with many of the recipes in this book, feel free to add and subtract the things you love or love less.

2 x 250 g punnets of cherry tomatoes, diced into 1 cm pieces

80 g (½ cup) capers, drained

80 g (½ cup) pitted kalamata olives, finely diced

2 garlic cloves, crushed

1 long red chilli, finely chopped OR chilli flakes to taste (optional)

1 lightly packed cup roughly chopped flat-leaf parsley leaves OR torn basil leaves

Finely grated zest of 1 lemon

80–100 ml olive oil

Salt & freshly ground black pepper

400–500 g spaghettini

100 g (1 cup) finely grated parmesan (optional)

FEEDS 4–6

DFO / V / VGO

To make the sauce, combine the tommies, capers, olives, garlic, chilli (if using), parsley or basil, lemon zest and olive oil in a medium bowl and fold together. Add salt and pepper to taste.

Cook the pasta with a ratio of 1 tablespoon of salt to 1 litre (4 cups) of water until al dente – that is, until there is the slightest grain of rawness in the middle, which means it will cook to perfection with the residual heat in the time that you drain and mix in the sauce.

Mix the pasta with the sauce, and serve with the parmesan on the side for diners to help themselves.

On warm summer days, I leave the pasta to cool before mixing it with the sauce and serve it at room temperature.

Surprisingly, this keeps very well for a few days, refrigerated, but is then best eaten chilled – trust me! In fact, the melded juices of all the vegetables become the most heavenly umami liquor, which soaks into the pasta and also keeps it soft and slippery.

ENOKI, GARLIC SCAPES & MALT VINEGAR SAUCE

This simple dish can be served as a starter, canapé or shared dish to have with rice. I circulated it on the Jamface Crunch Club menu for many seasons because even mushroom haters will hoover it up. Texturally, the long stems create a crunchy rather than 'slimy' texture, which seems to be the thing that mushroom detesters complain most about. This sauce is fantastic on top of any blanched Asian veg – great for an instant green dish if you're in a hurry. For those avoiding carbs, you could tip all of this over a bed of silken tofu instead of rice – simply drain the tofu well in a colander for at least 15 minutes, then season with salt so it doesn't dilute the flavour of the sauce.

350 g enoki mushrooms, with 2 cm of the stem base sliced away, strands separated into smaller clumps

50 g (½ cup) 5 mm thick slices of garlic scapes/shoots (found at Asian grocers)

2 tablespoons fried shallots

MALT VINEGAR SAUCE

3 tablespoons vegetable oil

3 garlic cloves, crushed

3 tablespoons oyster sauce OR mushroom oyster sauce

2 tablespoons malt vinegar

FEEDS 2, OR 6 AS PART OF A SHARED MEAL

GF / DF / VGO

Blanch the enoki mushrooms and garlic scapes in boiling water for a mere few seconds. Drain well in a sieve, using the back of a ladle to press as much excess water out as you can. Place in a bowl and set aside.

To make the malt vinegar sauce, combine the vegetable oil and garlic in a small saucepan over medium–high heat and cook until the garlic is starting to turn golden, then remove from the stove immediately and rest until just warm. In a clean glass jar, combine the garlic oil, oyster sauce and malt vinegar, then shake until emulsified.

Pour the sauce over the blanched mushrooms and garlic scapes. Mix then finish with the fried shallots and serve immediately.

The sauce keeps well refrigerated in an airtight glass jar for up to 2 weeks.

MISO-GLAZED SALMON OR EGGPLANT WITH CRUNCHY GREENS

A little sweetness truly makes miso sing. This is a perfect 10-minute meal – 3 minutes to make the basting sauce and 7 minutes to cook the salmon. Meanwhile, boil the kettle, blanch the veg, zap the remaining sauce in the microwave to warm it, then pour this over the veg and rice, and dinner is done! If you enjoy salmon skin, I've included how to make the perfect crispy salmon skin at the end of the recipe.

4 x 200 g salmon fillets (skinless if you don't enjoy it) OR 2 eggplants, sliced in half lengthways

300 g sugar snap OR snow peas

2 bunches of broccolini

3 tablespoons chopped spring onion (optional)

Steamed rice, to serve

MISO SAUCE

180 g (⅔ cup) shiro (white) miso paste

140 g (⅔ lightly packed cup) brown sugar

160 ml (⅔ cup) mirin

120 ml light soy sauce OR tamari

2 tablespoons water

1½ tablespoons finely grated ginger (or peeled & pounded to a pulp with a mortar & pestle)

6 garlic cloves, crushed

FEEDS 4

GFO / DF / VGO

Preheat the oven to 150°C fan-forced on the grill setting.

Line a baking tray with baking paper and place the salmon fillets or eggplant halves on it. If you are using eggplant, score a lattice pattern deeply into the flesh with a paring knife, skin-side down.

To make the miso sauce, mix all the ingredients until combined, then spoon generously over each piece of salmon or eggplant. Grill on the second-top shelf for 7–10 minutes, spooning on more miso sauce every few minutes, until the salmon or eggplant is cooked through.

While the salmon or eggplant are cooking, bring a medium saucepan of salted water to the boil. Blanch the sugar snap or snow peas for a few seconds, then the broccolini for a bit longer – you want both to be crisp but not raw.

To serve, divide the salmon or eggplant and the green vegetables among four plates. Microwave the remaining sauce in a small bowl for about 40 seconds on high and pour it over the vegetables. Top with the spring onion, if using, and serve with steamed rice.

HOW TO MAKE PERFECT CRISPY SALMON SKIN

To remove the salmon skin, lay the fillet, skin-side down, on a chopping board, tease a little space between the skin and the flesh with a sharp knife, then position the blade in that space, parallel to the chopping board, with the blade facing away from you. Press down firmly on the edge of the skin to hold the fillet in place, then slide the knife away from your body to remove the skin.

To cook the skins, brush them on both sides with a smidgen of olive oil (too much creates smoke as more fat renders out of the skin). Season the skins then lay them in a flat single layer in a non-stick frying pan over medium–low heat. Cover them with a piece of baking paper, then place a slightly smaller frying pan on top to keep the skins flat. Cook until golden and crisp, about 15 minutes, turning them over at the halfway mark. When the skins are fresh off the heat they will seem a little floppy but will crisp up on cooling. Use as a garnish – they are fantastic with the Vegetarian Chawanmushi with Shiitake & Konyakku Bundles on page 142.

SALTY

LONE
RANGER

Cooking for one

THREE OMELETTES TO HAVE WITH RICE

Just in case you haven't noticed, I love eggs! They're so fantastic for speed and certainly better than falling prey to junk food. Here are three of my besties to whip up when you open the fridge and all you have staring back at you is a sad tub of leftover rice.

CANTONESE STIR-FRIED TOMATO & EGG

4–5 large eggs

1 tablespoon light soy sauce OR tamari, or to taste

Pinch of sugar

2 tablespoons olive oil

3 garlic cloves, crushed

3 tomatoes, diced into 2 cm pieces

1 tablespoon Shaoxing rice wine

Steamed rice, to serve

MAKES 2 MEALS' WORTH

GFO / DF / V

In a medium bowl, whisk together the eggs, soy sauce or tamari and sugar.

Combine the oil and garlic in a large non-stick frying pan over high heat and sauté until pale golden. Add the tomato and Shaoxing rice wine. Stir-fry for a few seconds, just for the tommies to warm through, then add the egg mixture. Leave the egg alone so the bottom has time to caramelise before you start flipping and chopping into it until cooked through. Serve with steamed rice. Also great with a few ladles of chicken stock for a soupy effect.

GREAT AUNTY KIM'S MINT OMELETTE

6 large eggs

1 tablespoon Shaoxing rice wine

1–2 tablespoons light soy sauce OR tamari

½ teaspoon sugar

1 tablespoon sesame oil

1 tablespoon olive oil

2 tablespoons finely shredded ginger

3 garlic cloves, crushed

4–5 heaped handfuls of mint leaves

Steamed rice, to serve

MAKES 2–3 MEALS' WORTH

GFO / DF / V

In a medium bowl, whisk together the eggs, Shaoxing rice wine, soy sauce or tamari and sugar.

Combine the sesame and olive oil, ginger and garlic in a large non-stick frying pan over high heat and sauté until pale golden. Add the mint and stir-fry for a few seconds – just long enough for the mint to wilt – then add the egg mixture. Leave the egg alone so the bottom has time to caramelise before you start flipping and chopping into it until cooked through. Serve with steamed rice. Also great with a few ladles of chicken stock for a soupy effect.

XAR'S CHARRED EGGPLANT OMELETTE

1 eggplant

2–3 eggs

1 tablespoon light soy sauce OR tamari

1 tablespoon olive oil

2 garlic cloves, crushed

Steamed rice, to serve

3 tablespoons kecap manis

1 teaspoon sriracha chilli sauce OR any garlic chilli sauce

MAKES 2 MEALS' WORTH
GFO / DF / V

Place the eggplant in a smoking cast-iron chargrill pan or on a naked gas hob (a little messy to clean though), turned to the highest temperature possible. Keep turning the eggplant until all parts of the skin are charred well. Cool until comfortable to handle, then peel away the skin, keeping the stem attached.

In a small bowl, whisk together the eggs and soy sauce or tamari.

Combine the oil and garlic in a small non-stick frying pan over high heat and sauté until pale golden. Pour this into the bowl with the egg mixture and whisk to combine. Grease the pan with a little more olive oil, then add the egg mixture. Quickly drape the eggplant on top, folding some of the partially cooked egg over it. Keep flipping until the egg is brown and cooked through. Serve on top of steamed rice with the kecap manis and a zig-zag of sriracha or garlic chilli sauce.

Clockwise from top left:
Great Aunty Kim's Mint Omelette,
Xar's Charred Eggplant Omelette and
Cantonese Stir-Fried Tomato & Egg

MUM'S MALAYSIAN SAMBAL LEMAK WITH LEFTOVER RICE, FRIED EGGS & CUCUMBER

When people ask me what my favourite meal is, I say this. For one, Mum always makes the sambal for me, which I love, but this kampung (village) style of eating, which is so wonderfully frugal, is something my Great Aunty Kim taught me to appreciate from a young age. I'm infinitely amazed at how just mixing the smallest dollop of sambal can inject such an explosion of flavour into a simple bowl of rice. The eggs are a cheap, easy-to-cook protein and the cukes are there for cooling. You could call it a cheaty nasi lemak, but with the simple additions of fried peanuts and ikan bilis (dried whitebait), you'd take it pretty close to the real deal.

Leftover rice, reheated in the microwave, to serve

2–3 fried OR hardboiled eggs

½ continental cucumber, diced into bite-sized chunks

Soy OR fish sauce, to taste

SAMBAL

20 g belachan (shrimp paste; found in the Asian section of supermarkets or at Asian grocers)

20–25 dried chillies*, snapped in half, then covered & soaked in freshly boiled water for 15 minutes (soaking water reserved)

3 long red chillies

125 ml (½ cup) vegetable oil

3 teaspoons tamarind paste

3 onions, cut into 4 mm thick slices

2 tablespoons caster sugar

FEEDS 1

GFO / DF

To make the sambal, blitz the belachan, dried chillies and their soaking water, and the fresh chillies in a mini** food processor or blender until smooth. Combine with the vegetable oil in a medium non-stick frying pan over medium heat and cook, stirring regularly, until caramelised to a deep red and fragrant – sinuses will be charging at this point! Turn off the heat, then stir in the tamarind paste, onion and sugar. Cool and store in an airtight container in the fridge for up to 2 months.

To serve, mix the rice, eggs, cucumber, as much sambal as you can handle and a dash of soy or fish sauce. Taste and add more seasoning if needed.

*When you are buying dried chillies, the larger the chilli, the milder the heat. I often play around with combinations of large and small for my desired heat level. You can also shake the seeds out to temper the volatility.

**Mini because the chillies will only break down to a smooth paste in a smaller cavity.

FERMENTED BEAN CURD & LETTUCE STIR-FRY

I once cooked a Buddhist vegetarian dish for the late Antonio Carluccio using fermented bean curd and he remarked that it tasted like cheese, which kinduv blew my mind because it's true. Vegos and vegans, this is a fantastic seasoning alternative for you – it's salty, spicy, a little sharp and has tonnes of depth. This dish is something my Great Aunty Kim makes when she is fasting at certain times in the Buddhist calendar, and one I love to eat with rice when I'm craving simplicity. This recipe also works very well with kang kung (water spinach) or mixed mushrooms.

2–3 tablespoons olive oil

2–3 garlic cloves, crushed

1 tablespoon shredded ginger

1 long red chilli, finely sliced

4 baby gem lettuces, leaves separated & rinsed (cos & iceberg are also good)

2 cubes of white fermented bean curd*, mashed with 1 tablespoon of the fermenting liquid

1–2 tablespoons Shaoxing rice wine

2 teaspoons light soy sauce OR tamari

¼ teaspoon sugar

Steamed rice, to serve

MAKES 2 MEALS' WORTH
GFO / DF / VG

Combine the olive oil, garlic, ginger and chilli in a large non-stick frying pan over medium–high heat and sauté until pale golden. Add the lettuce leaves, fermented bean curd, Shaoxing rice wine, soy sauce or tamari and sugar. Stir-fry for only seconds until the lettuce leaves have barely wilted and the fermented bean curd has coated the leaves. Serve hot with steamed rice.

*Fermented bean curd, or tofu, comes in both white and red varieties. You can find it at Asian grocers.

'Don't hold onto things
too tightly – whatever flows, flows,
whatever blows, blows. Find ways
to embrace the unexpected. So many
times when something didn't take off,
I've later realised that other doors
were being opened for me but
I wasn't paying attention.'

Weeding around cacti can be a dangerous affair. Make a tunnel with old cardboard to act as protective walls, then weed away!

SPICED PORK CHOPS WITH CHARRED PEARS

This is one of those beautifully concise meals that I wanted this book to be all about. Easy as and utterly delicious! The combination of light spices, browned butter and sweetness of the fortified wine served with caramelised wedges of pear and peppery watercress, irrefutably belong together.

2 x not-too-thick pork cutlets

1 tablespoon olive oil

25 g butter

2–3 just-ripe pears OR persimmons, peeled & cut into 4–6 wedges

90 ml Pedro Ximénez sherry OR Madeira

MARINADE

2 tablespoons olive oil

2 garlic cloves, crushed

½ teaspoon chilli powder

½ teaspoon ground cumin

½ teaspoon ground coriander

½ teaspoon salt, or to taste

Freshly ground black pepper

Zest of ½ lemon

SALAD

2 handfuls of watercress OR rocket

2 teaspoons olive oil

Juice of 1 small lemon

Salt, to taste

MAKES 2 MEALS' WORTH

GF

Combine all the marinade ingredients in a bowl and mix well.

Place the pork cutlets on a plate, pour the marinade over the top and use a spoon to spread it evenly on all the surfaces of the pork. Cover with cling wrap and refrigerate for 15–20 minutes.

Heat the olive oil and butter in a heavy-based stainless steel frying pan over medium–high heat until foaming. Add the pork cutlets (reserve the marinade) and pear or persimmon. Cook the pork on each side until nicely browned, then turn the cutlets on their sides to sear and render out some of the fat. Turn the fruit so all sides are nicely caramelised but still firm enough to easily handle (it will be ready sooner than the pork).

Transfer the pork and fruit to a plate and pour the Pedro Ximénez or Madeira into the frying pan to deglaze. Add the remaining marinade and bring to the boil, then immediately pour the sauce over the pork and fruit.

To make the salad, combine all the ingredients in a medium mixing bowl, toss gently with clean hands and serve with the pork and fruit.

MIXED MUSHROOM & KALE STIR-FRY WITH NORI & LEMON

My favourite way to eat most days of the week is what I call 'almost vego'. I love the 'meatiness' of the mushrooms and kale, then the nori and oyster sauce really fill in the umami gaps. Add a hit of lemon and the whole thing comes alive. A brilliant dish to eat on its own if you go easy on the seasoning, otherwise I love to eat it with a small serving of brown rice.

1 tablespoon olive oil

30 g butter

3 garlic cloves, crushed

450 g mixed Asian mushrooms (enoki, shimeji, shiitake, baby oysters, king oysters – or regular white ones are also fine), torn into similar-sized pieces

4–5 large dried shiitake mushrooms, soaked in freshly boiled water for 30 minutes, drained (optional)

½–1 teaspoon dried chilli flakes OR 1 long red chilli, finely sliced

Handful of cloud ear fungus (dried black fungus; found at Asian grocers) soaked in plenty of cool water for 15 minutes, drained & hard parts torn off & discarded

1 small bunch of kale, leaves stripped from stalks, torn into bite-sized pieces

2 handfuls of flat-leaf parsley leaves

3 tablespoons oyster sauce OR mushroom oyster sauce, or to taste

1 teaspoon freshly ground black pepper

2–3 tablespoons lemon juice, or to taste

Steamed rice, to serve

1 nori sheet, finely shredded with scissors

MAKES 2–3 MEALS' WORTH

GF / VO

Combine the olive oil, butter and garlic in a large non-stick frying pan over medium–high heat. As soon as the garlic is fragrant, but not coloured, throw in the mushies and cook until there is some caramelisation. The easiest way to do this is to spread the mushrooms evenly across the pan and allow them to cook, without stirring, for about 2 minutes. If you are worried thicker mushrooms aren't cooking through, add a little splash of water to encourage steaming.

Add the chilli, cloud ear fungus, kale, parsley, oyster or mushroom sauce, pepper and lemon juice to taste. Toss for a few seconds to combine, then serve over steamed rice. Garnish with the nori at the very last minute.

FLATHEAD WITH BURNT BUTTER, LEMON & CAPER SAUCE

This is my favourite way to eat fish – uncluttered so you can taste every ingredient.

2 x 200 g flathead fillets OR any white fish you like

Salt & freshly ground black pepper

2 tablespoons olive oil

50 g butter

45 g (¼ cup) capers

Finely grated zest & juice of 1 lemon

GREEN BEANS & ALMONDS

250 g stringless green beans

1 garlic clove, peeled & bashed to split it a little

2 tablespoons lemon juice

Good glug of olive oil

Handful of roasted almonds, roughly chopped

Salt & freshly ground black pepper

MAKES 2 MEALS' WORTH

GF

Allow the fish to come to room temperature – about 10 minutes – then season on both sides.

Meanwhile, to prepare the beans, blanch them for a mere few seconds in salted boiling water, then immediately plunge into a bowl of cool water so they stay crisp and vibrantly green. Drain and transfer to a bowl, then toss with the garlic, lemon juice, olive oil, almonds, salt and pepper.

Heat the olive oil in a non-stick frying pan over medium–high heat and pan-fry the fish on both sides until cooked through. If I were to tell you how to achieve perfect 'doneness' here, it would take half a page, so I implore you to do what I did when I once had no idea, which is to pay the fish a lot of attention, and do things like prod or insert a paring knife at its thickest part for a sneaky peek, then make a judgement call. Just remember the residual heat will keep cooking the fish on resting, so account for this. Hopefully you have a bit of caramelisation on the flesh. And yes, skinless fillets are particularly hard to cook in a sexy single piece, so don't fall apart if it's not picture perfect, especially with oddly shaped, old-mate flathead.

Place the cooked fillets on serving plates, then throw the butter and capers in the pan. Allow the butter to brown (I like mine deep and toasty), then squeeze in the lemon juice. Give the pan a good scraping with a wooden spoon or plastic spatula, to get all that caramelised goodness into the sauce, and allow to simmer for a few seconds so it concentrates. At the very last minute add the zest so it stays beautifully bright in flavour, then pour the sauce over the fish.

Serve immediately with a side of the green beans and almonds.

SALTY

HANDMADE

Nourish and meditate

SARDINIAN CULURGIÒNE WITH BURNT SAGE BUTTER

Okay, firstly, even though I unabashedly gleam with pride for teaching myself how to make these from watching a YouTube tutorial, PLEASE ignore the pleating. I desperately want you to taste these wondrous pockets of potato perfection, so just seal the dumplings however you see fit. No matter how hideous they may look, know you are doing right by the universe for attempting something out of your comfort zone for the sake of flavour and helping perpetuate important cultural lessons!

POTATO FILLING

3 desiree potatoes, peeled & quartered (half sweet potato is also delicious)

100 g (1 cup) finely grated parmesan OR pecorino

Pinch or two of finely grated nutmeg

2–3 tablespoons finely shredded mint leaves

1 egg

Salt & freshly ground black pepper

DOUGH

300 g semolina

Plain flour, for dusting

BURNT SAGE BUTTER

100 g unsalted butter

10 sage leaves

Finely grated zest & juice of ½ small lemon, or to taste

FEEDS 2

v

To make the potato filling, steam the potatoes until tender, then press through a potato ricer. If you don't have a potato ricer, mash thoroughly with a fork. Add the remaining ingredients and stir to combine. The filling should be firm enough to easily roll into balls. Taste and season with salt and pepper. Add more cheese, nutmeg or mint if you like! Roll the mixture into heaped teaspoon-sized balls (a tad smaller than a golfball).

To make the dough, in a medium bowl, mix the semolina with enough warm water to knead it into a pliable dough. Add more rather than less water at the beginning as the semolina will soak it up rapidly. (It's easier to add semolina to an over-wet dough than to add more water to a dry dough.)

Once the dough gathers into a ball, knead for about 1 minute or until it's smooth and pliable and doesn't stick to the bench, without the help of flour. Run the dough through a pasta maker* on the thickest setting – #1 notch, then #2 notch and #3 notch – dusting with flour when necessary. Fold the pasta into thirds and repeat the process three more times. You will feel the texture stiffen and become smoother. On the final run, take it to #3, then cut out as many circles as you can with a round 8 cm pastry cutter. Gather the excess dough and continue to re-roll and cut out as many circles as possible. Dust the circles with flour and rest between sheets of baking paper on a baking tray covered with a damp tea towel.

To stuff the culurgiòne, place a ball of the potato filling in a circle of pasta, then seal the edge well, squeezing any air pockets out while you press the edge together. For the traditional pleating, which creates beautiful tear drop–shaped dumplings with wheat frond–patterned seams, you'll have to consult YouTube (my description would be an ineffectual five-page affair that leaves you still scratching your noggin). Place the dumpling on some well-floured baking paper, then repeat with the remaining dough and filling.

To make the burnt sage butter, melt the butter in a small saucepan over high heat until brown, add the sage leaves (be careful, they get a bit spitty) and cook until crisp, then immediately add the lemon zest and juice.

To cook the dumplings, lower them into a saucepan of salted boiling water. When they float, scoop them out and place them directly on a serving plate. Pour the burnt sage butter over the dumplings and serve immediately.

*If you don't have a pasta maker, roll the dough out until 1 mm thick on a floured surface.

MAMA YEOW'S SWEET PORK BUNS

I know these are madly cute but, if you're not experienced with yeast, I'm going to advise you to make these without the faces first. The ears and snout are incredibly fiddly and the delay can mean you overprove the buns, which is not worth it! Once you've mastered the recipe, you'll understand where the critical points in the proving are and see how the faces can fit with your time management. These instantly transport me to moments spent in front of the wistful gaze of Grandma Yeow encouraging me and my brother to inhale yet more of the buns, among many other treats she had prepared specially for our visit.

2 tablespoons olive oil

1 large onion, diced into 1 cm pieces

500 g lean belly pork, diced into 1 cm pieces

1 tablespoon light soy sauce

1 tablespoon dark caramel soy sauce (found at Asian grocers)

70 g sugar

¾ teaspoon salt

1 teaspoon white pepper

1–2 teaspoons wheaten cornflour (optional)

2 tablespoons water (optional)

BUN DOUGH

1 teaspoon dry yeast

1 tablespoon caster sugar

300 ml warm water

360 g plain flour

¾ teaspoon baking powder

25 g caster sugar

½ teaspoon salt

1 tablespoon vegetable oil

MAKES 12

DF

Combine the olive oil and onion in a medium non-stick frying pan over high heat and cook until the onion is soft and translucent. Add the pork and stir-fry until cooked through. Stir in the light and dark caramel soy sauce, sugar, salt and pepper and cook until sticky and caramelised. If there's a lot of excess oil, rest the frying pan, tilted, to see if you can get it to pool to one side where you can scoop or dab it away with paper towel. If the sauce needs thickening and you feel it might dry the meat to keep cooking, mix the cornflour and water, add it to the pan and cook over medium heat until it thickens and coats the pork well. Spread on a plate and cool completely before using.

To make the bun dough, stir the dry yeast and sugar with HALF the warm water in a bowl. Cover and rest for about 10 minutes or until the surface is foamy. Combine with the remaining warm water and dough ingredients in a stand mixer fixed with the dough hook attachment, and mix on the lowest speed for 2 minutes. Transfer the dough to a well-oiled bowl, cover and allow to rise until it doubles in volume, about 40 minutes.

Punch down the dough and divide into 12 even balls*. Roll each ball with a rolling pin into a 5 mm thick circle. Place a tablespoon of the pork mixture in the middle of a dough circle. Gather the edge into the middle and pinch to seal, then place seam-side down on a 10 cm square of baking paper in a bamboo steaming basket**. Repeat with the remaining filling and dough. Put the lid on the steamer, then drape a damp tea towel over the lid and allow the filled buns to prove again until doubled in size, about 20 minutes.

Steam for 5–7 minutes on a rolling boil. They can be frozen for up to a month and refreshed with a 10-minute steam. Serve hot or at room temperature.

*When you graduate to doing the faces, you will need an extra golf ball–sized piece of dough. As for how, I have faith you can figure it out. Use a skewer for the holes and also to secure the ears and snout.

**For calculating how much real estate you'll need in your bamboo steamer, the buns will each wind up about 8 cm in diameter.

Poof we brought from
Malaysia which was a gift
from Egyptian neighbours
we had for many years

PORK & KIMCHI DUMPLINGS
WITH THAI CHILLI JAM

Pro chefs are known for being cowboy eaters. When my mate Scottie Pickett suggested we eat my kimchi dumplings with Thai chilli jam, I was convinced it was a tragic white man move, but even more annoying is that it worked so well. I should have known sweet and shrimpy would be great friends of pork and kimchi. However, please go to the effort of finding a respected Thai brand of chilli jam from an Asian grocer or it might not be an adventure worth having. Also, if the steam-fry method seems too difficult for you, you can simply boil the dumplings (they are ready when they float).

Olive oil, for cooking

3 tablespoons Chinkiang vinegar (found in the Asian section of supermarkets or at Asian grocers)

2 tablespoons finely shredded ginger

Jar of good-quality Thai chilli jam (found at Asian grocers)

DUMPLING SKINS

150 g (1 cup) plain flour, plus extra for dusting

About 110 ml freshly boiled water

PORK & KIMCHI FILLING

280 g medium-coarse, moderately fatty pork OR chicken mince

200 g (1 cup) kimchi, squeezed savagely & roughly chopped

1 tablespoon finely chopped ginger

⅓ cup finely sliced spring onion OR Chinese chives

⅛ teaspoon white pepper

1½ tablespoons light soy sauce

1 tablespoon Shaoxing rice wine

2–3 teaspoons sesame oil

FEEDS 2 AS A MAIN

DF

To make the dumpling skins, place the flour in a medium bowl, make a well in the middle and, using chopsticks or a fork, mix in enough of the boiling water to bind the flour into a rough ball. When the dough has cooled a little and safe to touch, switch to using your hands and knead into a pliable ball – it shouldn't need flour to prevent it from sticking to the benchtop.

Divide the dough into two pieces and roll into cylinders 3 cm in diameter. Anytime the dough feels sticky, dust with more flour. Slice the cylinders into 2 cm thick discs, then flatten them with the palm of your hand. Toss them with plenty of flour, then cover with an overturned bowl to stop them from drying out.

To make the pork and kimchi filling, combine all the ingredients in a bowl and mix well with a wooden spoon or clean hands.

Use a dumpling rolling pin to roll out the skins until they are about 1 mm thick – roll from the outer edge towards the centre of the circle, as this helps maintain an even circle. Place about 1 teaspoon of the filling in the middle. Crimp the edges of the dumplings together to seal. When crimping, pleat only one side of the wrapper – this will pull the dumpling into a traditional crescent shape. If this sounds too difficult, simply pinch the edges to seal well, but rest the dumpling on a well-floured baking tray with the seam pointing upwards so there's a nice flat bottom for crisping up.

To cook the dumplings, grease a large non-stick frying pan well with olive oil, then arrange the dumplings in a single layer with at least 1 cm of space between them. Fill the pan with about 6 mm of water and shake the pan very gently to make sure the dumplings slide easily. Cover and simmer over medium heat until the water is nearly all evaporated, shaking the pan occasionally to loosen the dumpling bottoms so they don't stick. Remove the lid and allow the bottoms to crisp up to a golden brown.

To serve, turn the dumplings upside down so the crispy bottoms are facing up or you will steam the crunch away! Combine the Chinkiang vinegar and ginger and divide between two dipping bowls. Add a heaped dessertspoon of Thai chilli jam but don't mix it together so diners can use both condiments as they please. Serve with the hot dumplings.

'When you're feeling under the weather or like a bug is coming on, pound a 5–10 cm piece of scrubbed ginger (depends how spicy your palate can manage), skin on, until it splits and is a little flattened. Boil for a maximum of 10 minutes (otherwise all the good stuff will lose potency) with 2 cups of water and sip slowly with a little honey before bedtime. It does the trick for me every time!'

For a super-light saucepan lid that helps contain little wooden spoon messes after you've stirred the pot, I love to use beautifully dinged and chipped enamel plates from thrift stores.

COLD VEGETARIAN DAN DAN NOODLES

I promise this will be one of the most spectacular things you will ever eat – an explosive experience of cool, toasty, nutty, numbing, fiery, sharp, sweet and salty all at once, coating the best noodles you've ever tasted because YOU'VE made them. The authentic flavour and mouthfeel of the noodles are due to the kansui, or alkaline water, but it's something you won't miss if it's not familiar to you, so don't fret if you have to omit it. This recipe requires a pasta maker with a 2–3 mm noodle cutter, if possible. Otherwise roll the dough out very thinly with lots of flour, roll it up and slice very finely, then toss generously with more flour to keep the strands nicely separated.

SZECHUAN CHILLI OIL

250 ml (1 cup) vegetable oil

2 tablespoons Szechuan peppercorns

1 small cinnamon stick

2 star anise

40 g (½ cup) dried chilli flakes

DRESSING

3 tablespoons tahini

3 tablespoons light soy sauce

2 teaspoons Chinkiang vinegar (found in the Asian section of supermarkets or at Asian grocers)

2 teaspoons caster sugar

½ teaspoon Chinese five-spice powder

½ teaspoon ground Szechuan peppercorns

125 ml (½ cup) Szechuan Chilli Oil (see above)

2 garlic cloves, crushed

STIR-FRY

2 tablespoons vegetable OR olive oil

3 garlic cloves, finely chopped

2 cm piece of ginger, finely chopped

12 large dried shiitake mushrooms, soaked in freshly boiled water for 30 minutes, drained & sliced into 3 mm pieces

Pinch of white pepper

½ teaspoon Chinese five-spice powder

2 teaspoons dark soy sauce

1 teaspoon light soy sauce

1 tablespoon Shaoxing rice wine

HANDMADE WHEAT NOODLES

400 g (2⅔ cups) plain flour, plus extra for dusting

2 teaspoons kansui (also called lye or alkaline water – not the health-style alkaline water designed for drinking; found at Asian grocers)

TO SERVE

80 g (½ cup) salted roasted peanuts

60 g (½ cup) chopped spring onion

½ cup roughly chopped coriander, including stalks

1 bunch of choy sum, sliced into 10 cm lengths, blanched in boiling water & drained

FEEDS ABOUT 4

DF / VG

To make the Szechuan chilli oil, combine all the ingredients in a small saucepan over medium heat. Stir occasionally, until they become toasty and fragrant. Remove from the heat when you see bubbles start to emerge.

To make the dressing, combine all the ingredients in a clean glass jar and shake until mixed thoroughly.

To make the stir-fry, combine the vegetable or olive oil, garlic and ginger in a small frying pan over medium–high heat and cook until golden and fragrant. Add the shiitake mushroom, white pepper, five-spice powder, dark and light soy sauces and Shaoxing rice wine and stir to combine, then remove from the heat and set aside to cool.

To make the noodles, combine the flour, kansui* and enough warm water to knead the flour into a pliable ball of dough – if you have the right amount of moisture, the dough should not stick to your work surface even without a dusting of flour. Knead by hand for about 5 minutes or in a stand mixer, fitted with the dough hook attachment, on the lowest speed for 2 minutes. Knead by hand into a ball and divide into four equal portions. Using a rolling pin, roll out each piece of dough until it is about 5 mm thick. Cover three pieces of the dough with a damp tea towel while you work with one. Dust the dough generously with flour, then pass it through the #1 setting on the pasta maker. Pass it through the #2 setting, then the #3 setting, dusting well with flour each time. Fold into thirds and repeat the process three more times. On the final roll, pass the dough all the way through to the #5 setting, dust well, then pass through the noodle cutter and toss gently with generous amounts of flour so the strands don't stick. Repeat with the remaining pieces of dough.

Bring a saucepan of salted water to the boil (1 tablespoon of salt to 1 litre (4 cups) of water). Lower each serve of noodles into the pan individually, agitating them with chopsticks once they hit the boiling water. When the noodles float to the surface, scoop them out with a spider ladle and transfer to a large bowl of cool water. Drain in a sieve briefly before placing into serving bowls.

In a medium bowl, combine 125 ml (½ cup) of the noodle cooking water with the dressing and whisk until smooth. Top each bowl with 3 tablespoons of the dressing and one-quarter of the stir-fry and garnishes. Allow your guests to mix their own noodles.

*Please do not handle the kansui straight as it can be very irritating to your skin.

HANDMADE SEMOLINA CAVATELLI

This is my favourite pasta to make and eat. The shape and texture catches plenty of sauce and has the most satisfying bite. If you don't have a proper gnocchi paddle, you can MacGyver it with a sushi mat! Serve with Cassie Lee's No-Cook Tomato Sauce (page 24), Anchovy Butter & Fresh Tomato (page 167) or Zen's Creamy Zucchini & Ancho Pasta Sauce (page 174).

400 g fine semolina

Flour, for dusting

Salt

FEEDS 4

DF / VG

Place the semolina in a medium bowl and add enough warm water to gather the contents into a pliable dough. At first, err on the side of the dough looking wetter than needed, as the semolina is very thirsty and will soak the water up. (Also, it's much easier to knead more semolina, rather than water, into the dough.) Knead enthusiastically for about 5 minutes, then cover with an upturned bowl and rest for about 20 minutes.

To make the cavatelli, roll a golf ball–sized chunk of semolina dough into a 1 cm thick noodle. Cut into 2 cm pieces, then dust well with plenty of flour. Position a gnocchi paddle or sushi mat with its lines running vertically towards you. Place the long side of a piece of the cut pasta across the grain of the paddle, then, holding a pastry scraper at about a 40-degree angle and holding the paddle with your non-dominant hand, press and drag against the pasta starting from one edge to the other so it rolls into something that resembles a ridged log. Some like to press the pasta away from their body and some towards – whatever works best for you. Repeat until all the pasta is made.

Bring a large saucepan of salted water to the boil (1 tablespoon of salt to 1 litre (4 cups) of water). Add the pasta and cook until it floats to the surface, then use following whichever sauce recipe you have chosen.

'Take time to create beautiful spaces even if you have very little. I've always had a very strong nesting impulse because I've felt like an outsider for much of my life. The spaces I dwell in, the objects I surround myself with, have been a way to build my identity that didn't rely on others. I'm not talking exxy or fancy – it's largely items from church bazaars and local thrift stores. For me, it's been a kind of self-care, crafting an environment that feeds healthy, hopeful thoughts and inspires my creativity. My other tip for decorating, whether indoors or when designing a garden, is to always build your aesthetic over time. Just get by with what you need at first, then slowly collect things that have meaning to fill existing hollows when you can afford it. You also need to live in the space and allow it to tell you what it needs for function and flow. Doing it impatiently, all at once, will reveal just that.'

To get stains off pale porous surfaces ...

Rub a small amount of toothpaste onto the affected area in a circular motion, then wipe away with a damp towel. The small particles act as a very fine abrasive and the bicarb absorbs the stain.

HAND-ROLLED SUSHI

Feeling like sushi but can't be arsed with the fiddliness of it all? Go hand-rolled and let the troops feed themselves! The kids have a ball because they get to be boss of their own dinner and you get the night off slaving over a hot stove – it's a good deal. Vegos and vegans, you can omit the seafood and tobiko.

440 g (2 cups) koshihikari rice (found in supermarkets) OR medium-grain rice

750 ml (3 cups) water

2 tablespoons sushi seasoning, or to taste

8 nori sheets, quartered

½ continental cucumber, quartered lengthways, seeds sliced away & cut into long batons

1 avocado, flesh scooped out & cut into long batons

24 cooked, peeled prawns OR any cooked protein OR raw sashimi-worthy seafood of choice

Small bottle of Japanese mayonnaise

About 30 g (⅓ cup) tobiko (found in the freezer section of Asian grocers)

TO SERVE

125 ml (½ cup) Japanese soy sauce OR tamari

2 teaspoons wasabi paste

FEEDS 4

GFO / DF / VGO

Combine the rice and water in a medium non-stick saucepan and bring to the boil. Cook, covered, for 10–15 minutes on the lowest simmer possible, until no liquid is visible but the surface of the rice is dotted with large pits. Turn the heat off and allow the rice to rest, covered, for 15 minutes, then add the sushi seasoning and fold it in using a rice paddle or rubber spatula until well combined. Cover to keep warm until needed.

To assemble one of these puppies, grab a golf ball–sized amount of rice with wet fingers (to stop the rice from sticking; a small bowl of water next to every person is a good idea). Continue to use your fingers to spread the rice thinly onto a square of nori. Load it up with your ingredients of choice and roll into a cone shape or simply bring two sides together to cradle the fillings and munch away ... with soy and wasabi for dipping of course!

SALTY

CROWD PLEASERS

Just YUM!

VEGETARIAN CHAWANMUSHI WITH SHIITAKE & KONYAKKU BUNDLES

If you can imagine the texture of the most silken crème caramel, but savoury, you have chawanmushi. Truly everyone loves this dish – babies, tots, oldies, foodies and non-foodies, people from all cultures. It's the purest kind of comfort and the flavours, mellow and unobtrusive. The thing that's really fun about it is you can embed whatever secret you want within – perhaps a trio of succulent seafood, such as squid tentacles, a prawn and a few pieces of cockle meat. The success of this dish relies on observation and patience. If it takes too long to cook, you might need to raise the heat a tad higher. If the custard puffs up, the heat has been too aggressive. But don't stress too much because it will still be delish, if only texturally compromised – practice makes perfect! And if you have any leftovers, you can simply microwave them to reheat.

4 eggs

370 ml plant-based chicken-flavoured stock OR water

1 tablespoon Shaoxing rice wine

1 teaspoon light soy sauce OR tamari

Good pinch each of white pepper & caster sugar

8–12 konyakku noodle bundles*, drained

4 dried shiitake mushrooms (soaked in freshly boiled water for 30 minutes, drained & finely sliced)

TOPPINGS

1 teaspoon sesame oil

4 teaspoons light soy sauce OR tamari

2 spring onions, finely sliced

80 ml (⅓ cup) peanut oil

FEEDS 4 AS A GENEROUS STARTER

GFO / DF / V

In a medium bowl whisk together the eggs, stock, Shaoxing rice wine, soy sauce or tamari, white pepper and sugar until just combined – you don't want too much aeration. Cover and set aside at room temperature.

Divide the konyakku bundles among four ramekins, then divide the mushroom and the egg mixture evenly among them. Place the ramekins in a large bamboo steamer** and steam for 20–30 minutes on low heat. Make sure the bowls are low enough to be completely covered by the basket lid and don't be afraid to peek under the cover a few times to check for 'doneness'. The custard should be set flat with no air bubbles and not wobbly.

When they come out of the steamer, top each ramekin with ¼ teaspoon of sesame oil, 1 teaspoon of light soy sauce or tamari and 1 teaspoon of sliced spring onion. Heat the peanut oil in a small saucepan until smoking then, standing well away, spoon 1 tablespoon of the hot oil over each bowl. Be careful as it will spit quite violently. Serve immediately.

*These are most commonly used in hotpot and can be bought vac-packed in liquid from Asian grocers.

**Don't use a metal steamer as the condensation will fall back into the custards and prevent them from setting properly.

'All your experiences, whether positive or negative, define you.
Each state needs to exist to give the other meaning. If things were good all the time,
you'd be desensitised to joy – this is the ebb and flow of life.'

'When it comes to finding a career with stamina, I have absolute faith in this principle: steer in the general direction of things you love to do, and take pride in your work. I've never cut a linear, tidy path. It's been more of a meander with loads of hard work in between. Overnight success is a myth.'

MARGARET'S CURRY CASHEW SLAW

My late ex-mother-in-law, Margaret, used to make this retro salad a lot. It was always meat 'n' three at the Phipps's (which I was totally into because I never got it growing up) – three steamed veg or three salads – and this one was a crowd favourite. Great with fried chicken!

¼ green OR red cabbage, finely sliced

1 carrot, peeled & coarsely grated

1 small white OR red onion, finely sliced

2 spring onions, finely sliced

80 g (½ cup) roasted cashew nuts

40 g (⅓ cup) sultanas

CURRY MAYO DRESSING

2 tablespoons whole-egg mayonnaise

1 teaspoon dijon mustard

1 teaspoon curry powder

1 teaspoon crushed garlic

80 ml (⅓ cup) apple cider vinegar

2 tablespoons milk of your choice

80 ml (⅓ cup) honey

FEEDS ABOUT 8

GF / DFO / V

Combine all the curry mayo dressing ingredients in a clean glass jar and shake until well mixed.

Place all the salad ingredients in a bowl without mixing.

Pour the dressing over the salad and gently combine with salad tossers. Serve with whatever you like!

This keeps well, refrigerated overnight, covered. In fact, the dressing penetrates deeper into the vegetables, which makes them even tastier the next day!

Colander that's been with the Yeow family for 37 years ↘

THYME, LEMON & GARLIC CHICKEN WITH PAN-FRIED POTATOES

This is one of my favourite 'can't think what to cook' meals and – of the many things in my repertoire – the one that's most requested by friends and family. There's nothing not to love about it, just the most unpretentious kind of yum, so it's very handy for feeding fussy eaters.

4 chicken breast fillets, sliced on a steep diagonal into 3–4 medallions

2 tablespoons thyme leaves

Handful of flat-leaf parsley leaves, roughly chopped

2–3 garlic cloves, crushed

Finely grated zest of 1 lemon

80 ml (⅓ cup) lemon juice

2–3 tablespoons olive oil, plus extra for frying

1 teaspoon salt

Freshly ground black pepper, to taste

PAN-FRIED POTATOES

1 kg potatoes, skins left on

125 ml (½ cup) olive oil

50 g butter

Salt & freshly ground black pepper

FEEDS 4

GF

In a large saucepan of salted water, boil the potatoes until tender, then drain in a colander. Cool briefly, then press on each potato with the palm of your hand so it splits into several pieces.

Place the chicken in a large bowl. In a small bowl, mix the thyme, parsley, garlic, lemon zest and juice, olive oil, salt and pepper, then pour this mixture over the chicken. Use a spoon to flip the chicken pieces in the marinade until well coated. Cover and refrigerate for about 10 minutes.

Add 2–3 tablespoons of olive oil to a large, non-stick frying pan over medium–high heat, add the chicken (reserve the marinade) and pan-fry until golden on each side and cooked through. Transfer the cooked chicken to a large serving plate. Pour the reserved marinade into the frying pan and bring to a simmer. Scrape the bottom of the pan with a wooden spoon or plastic spatula to release all the caramelisation. Pour the sauce over the chicken, then cover to keep warm.

To finish the potatoes, heat the olive oil and butter in a large frying pan until melted. Working in batches, add the potato and cook over medium–high heat until golden and crispy. Season with salt and pepper, then serve hot alongside the chicken.

Short-arse Batman

DIRT & DANDELIONS
(Thoughts on why gardening saves me)

In many ways, I'm a terrible gardener. My method is by trial and play. I confess to sometimes having favourite children that I will tend to more attentively, depending on what seems to be more obedient in its pre-determined habit. I'm hopelessly forgiving of the chaos that ensues from allowing things to self-seed. And it winds up looking like this ... entitled sprays of delicate coriander or pink cosmos happily growing right in the middle of the gravel pathways between the veggie beds and a wild clover that most consider a weed taking over prime real estate, even drowning out the light for some legit spots in the bed where the spring onions and corn want to grow. To these wayward types, I will actually utter words of encouragement: 'How clever you are to find a sweet spot that's in the way of EVERYONE!'.

In short, I'm a sucker for beauty, whether weed or deliberately cultivated, and my endless fascination with the stoicism of nature means things only grew in tidy rows for the first season we built and planted the garden, but haven't, nor ever will, again. One year a pumpkin sprang out of one of the most inhospitable spots in the backyard. With a little detective work, I suspect it was seeded from meals I've fed to Rhino and Tim, if you get the drift, as I've never planted pumpkins nor any veg nor used compost in that part of the backyard. I was dead curious to see, without watering it, how tenaciously expansive its triffid-like tentacles would stretch, and how much fruit it might bear. I left it in total neglect until it covered my entire 36 m^2 backyard and bore about six very decent pumpkins. I mean, that's amazing, isn't it?

When I parted ways with the notion of a monotheistic religion, nature became my god. I can't help but be seduced by its beauty and resilience, sometimes its indiscriminate brutality. I find spirituality and wonder in the rhythms, geometry and symmetry ... the number of times I've been late for things because I made the mistake of wandering through the garden while getting to the car! All I need is to catch sight of a couple of stinkbugs mating precariously on top of a cactus or signs of an infant leaf teasing the soil surface (radish seeds planted 12 days ago, already making a path to sunlight and converting it to fruit). Or finding what was a burgeoning row of kale yesterday decimated by cabbage moth larvae this morning, leaving behind a veritable lacework of leaves. It's all amazing to me and I'm sucked into the garden vortex where everything else ceases to exist but me in these curious microcosms.

I could bang on forever, all the life lessons ... but here are some tips that seem to have worked very well for me, some of it despite what professional gardeners might advise (pros, avert your eyes).

1. **Strength in numbers.** Plant clusters of seedlings together to ensure the survival of at least one plant. It seems just one or two extra stems in the mix gives all the plants a little more resilience – if you plant on a warm day, a single skinny seedling often won't make it. With certain plants like thyme or flowers, I've often planted the entire punnet of six seedlings in the one spot. If they all thrive and get a bit out of control, deal with it then!

2. **If planting straight from seed,** when the seedlings seem strong enough (about 10 cm high), you can relocate plants and/or tidy up their positions, especially if more space is needed between the plants (called thinning), then water well after. They might look sad for a day but should perk up after the sun's gone down.

3. **Allow things to go to seed** even though it can look ugleh. When the plant is dried up, you can harvest the seeds to plant next year or share with friends, but my fave thing that happens here is that the wind takes the seeds where it wants and where they find a home is where they will thrive. I love the surprises that ensue when spring arrives and you find Mother Nature has already done some planting for you, often in spots that reveal she has a great sense of humour. Again, if any of these guys are in a bit of a silly spot, just make sure you dig with care and relocate them to a more ideal position.

4. **I never spray,** I just put it down to having to share with nature. Fruit trees I net. I've always found things like curly leaf on stone fruit trees seem to take care of themselves after a season or two.

5. **USE the instructions on the plant labels** and heed the position advice, such as full sun or part shade. However, the Aussie sun is mega intense, so if you can see that plants recommended to be in full sun are burning, erect a little shade cloth over the top. I find even the most robust of tomatoes can boil in unrelenting South Aussie summers.

6. **I like to plant equal parts flowers to veg,** with flowers around the borders of the veg beds, as they encourage pollinators to visit but also add colour and beauty.

7. **For the black thumbs, plant lots of succulents.** They're so forgiving, you don't need much water nor a memory TO water. Some even seem to only push out their vibrant alien flowers after feelings of abandonment. Back in my student days, I loved that I could pilfer just a few leaves from any succulent, stick it in average-quality dirt and, hey presto, I had grown something green.

8. **When it comes to gardening, you have to love it!** And by this I mean ALL of it, the good and the tedious parts in equal measure. I've learnt so much from weeding. If you can push past the annoyance, you will find it meditative. I always approach it like when I first learnt to draw a complex image using a grid – my art teacher explained that the idea is to not allow the entirety of the image to overwhelm you but only focus on one square of the grid at a time – before you know it, the individual squares are all joined up and you've drawn something you never thought possible. Weeding has also taught me that allowing nature to dictate my daily activities forces me into the natural order of things, which is a concept I live my life by. For instance, if it's rained, I know it can't wait, I must weed the day after while the ground is wet and wants to help me. I also quickly learnt that it's imperative to do your own dirty work. It keeps you humble and connected to the earth, but I also know my garden best so when I see a cluster of what seems to be the same infant leaves, I easily recognise that only two are weeds and among the others I can identify the beginning of violas, flat-leaf parsley, red spider mizuna or coriander. It's nothing short of joyful to be able to do this. It's fostering an intimacy with your garden that just can't be done if you're not watching closely. Unknowing eyes and hands would have yanked all of them out.

9. **Plant only what you need,** because it is overwhelming when things fruit all at once. Where I used to plant more food I now plant flowers because I've found beauty as much a source of joy as food is, but also for the happiness of bees. To be honest, when it comes to planting food, I stick to the basics – tomatoes, Italian and Thai basil, coriander (which self-seeds in perpetuity – convenient because it NEVER seems to work when you intentionally plant it), chillies, spring onions (I always keep the root after using and stick it into any empty patch I can find), cucumbers, zucchini, eggplants, beets, chard, strawberries, radishes and LOTS of herbs. In fact, herbs are almost my favourite thing to grow because I love their fragrance and ability to turn very plain meals into something a bit spesh. Among my faves are thyme (I grow enough to sink a ship because the bees dig it and I love how it influences the flavour of my honey), sage, pineapple sage, mint (PLEASE contain this – I didn't listen and it's become the bane of my existence), passionfruit daisy (beautiful for tea), lemon verbena, lemon balm, laksa leaf, bay leaf, curry leaf, chives, oregano and rosemary.

10. **I also have a border of fruit trees,** mainly stone fruit – apricot, nectarine, red and yellow peach, Santa Rosa and satsuma plum – but also pink lady apple, brown turkey fig, lemon, lime, Washington navel and Seville orange, passionfruit, feijoa and blueberry. As a general rule, when pruning fruit trees (also roses), try for a wine-glass shape, to allow sunlight to penetrate through the foliage to the fruit. For roses, it's for the leaves to aerate with ease and avoid mildew after rain.

11. **If anything's looking straggly,** treat it mean to keep it keen and cut it back to where it's looking good. A savage pruning can catalyse healthy growth. I always cut dead or dying flowers away to promote new growth.

12. **Mulch to help water retention** and keep the weeds at bay.

13. **Gardening is like home decorating** – it's wise to build the aesthetic slowly, observing what the space needs and what your needs are. Whenever I'm at the hardware store I'll buy a few plants to add interesting details to the garden.

14. **If you have the space, the ground is always better** than pots. Pots are volatile. If you forget to water, they are unforgiving, but in the ground, roots can search for water.

Feeling like a minuscule dot in the firmament is healthy. When I went through my miscarriage, it was the sobering thought that one-third of all pregnancies in the world go this way that comforted me. It was a why not me, rather than a why me, that saved me from my grief. Tragedy is indiscriminate. The less you personalise it, the easier it gets.

PRAWN & PORK BALLS, GLASS VERMICELLI IN FRAGRANT COCONUT SAUCE

This prawn and pork ball mixture can be stuffed into wonton wrappers and simmered in the sauce instead of being pan-fried and eaten with the glass vermicelli. The sauce is also fantastic to poach a piece of fish or whole prawns in, if you're avoiding carbs. Either way, this is a beautifully fragrant dish with plenty of South-East Asian 'tude. If you can't be arsed rolling the prawn and pork into balls, you can pan-fry it like mince, then tip it into the sauce – same same but different.

80 ml (⅓ cup) olive oil

3 garlic cloves, crushed

8 sprigs of curry leaves, leaves picked

3 cm piece of ginger, finely chopped

2 green scud chillies, finely chopped

2 teaspoons black mustard seeds

1–2 stalks of lemongrass, pounded with a pestle to flatten & split

400 ml tin coconut milk

1 litre (4 cups) chicken stock

3 tablespoons fish sauce

3 tablespoons lime juice

150 g glass vermicelli noodles, soaked in warm water for 5 minutes & drained

4 bunches of bok choy, halved or cut into bite-sized pieces

1 cup Vietnamese mint leaves (laksa leaves) OR roughly chopped coriander, including stalks

PRAWN & PORK BALLS

350 g prawn meat

400 g reasonably fatty coarse pork mince

2 tablespoons tapioca flour OR potato starch

1 tablespoon fish sauce

2 teaspoons sugar

¼ teaspoon white pepper

FEEDS 6

GF / DF

To make the prawn and pork balls, first pulse the prawn meat in a food processor until coarsley chopped. Scrape into a medium bowl. Next, blitz the pork mince in the food processor with the tapioca flour, fish sauce, sugar and white pepper until it turns into a paste. Add to the prawn meat and mix until well combined. Using wet hands or a small ice cream scoop, form into golf ball–sized balls, then place on a greased baking tray.

Heat 1 tablespoon of the olive oil in a large non-stick frying pan over high heat and brown the pork and prawn balls, turning them occasionally for even colour – they don't have be cooked through. Transfer to a plate.

Combine the remaining oil, the garlic, curry leaves, ginger, chilli and mustard seeds in the pan and stir-fry until fragrant but not coloured. Stir in the lemongrass, coconut milk, stock and fish sauce, then return the prawn and pork balls to the pan. Simmer until the prawn and pork balls are cooked through, then stir in the lime juice and glass vermicelli noodles.

To serve, place the bok choy at the bottom of each bowl. Ladle the soup, vermicelli and prawn and pork balls over the top, then garnish with the Vietnamese mint or coriander.

FAST BUTTER CHICKEN

I'm famous for my appalling time management, but occasionally it yields a delicious reward like this, which was born out of having to compress a longish recipe into very little time. BUT IT WORKED. Please don't let the long list of ingredients put you off because, once you read the method, you'll see most of it is dealt with in three steps. Be prepared to go carb cray on this because that sauce needs to be soaked up – hello rice and naan! Vegos can replace the chicken with a mixture of red lentils, kidney beans and peas.

1 small onion, quartered

2 garlic cloves, peeled

2 cm piece of ginger, roughly sliced

3 tablespoons water

50 g butter OR ghee

2 teaspoons ground coriander

2 teaspoons ground cumin

4 cloves

1 cinnamon stick

8 cardamon pods, bashed

Pinch of ground nutmeg

1 teaspoon garam masala

1–2 teaspoons chilli powder

1 teaspoon freshly ground black pepper

2 bay leaves

400 g tin crushed tomatoes

2 tablespoons tomato paste

100 g Greek yoghurt

200 ml cream

2 tablespoons honey OR maple syrup

1½ teaspoons salt

1 teaspoon sugar

700 g chicken thigh fillets, halved

TURMERIC RICE

20 g butter OR ghee

400 g (2 cups) basmati rice

¼ teaspoon ground turmeric

700 ml water

RAITA

390 g (1½ cups) Greek yoghurt

½ continental cucumber, coarsely grated

2 tablespoons lemon juice

¼ teaspoon sugar

½ teaspoon salt

FEEDS UP TO 7

GF / VO

To make the turmeric rice, melt the butter or ghee in a medium non-stick saucepan over medium heat. Mix in the rice and turmeric until combined, then the water. Boil for 10 minutes, then reduce the heat and simmer, covered, for another 10 minutes until there is no visible liquid left and there are finger-sized pits on the surface. Turn off the heat and rest, covered, for 15 minutes, then fluff with a rice paddle or rubber spatula. If you prefer, you can use the method for the Afghan-Style Rice on page 202, which is more traditional and has a lighter result.

If making the raita, mix all the ingredients in a bowl until combined. Cover and refrigerate until needed.

Blitz the onion, garlic, ginger and water in a blender or small food processor until it forms a paste.

Combine the butter or ghee, coriander, cumin, cloves and cinnamon in a large saucepan over medium heat and toast until fragrant. Add the onion paste and sauté for 4 minutes. Add the cardamom, nutmeg, garam masala, chilli powder, pepper and bay leaves and sauté for 1 minute. Stir in the remaining ingredients, then the chicken. Simmer for 10–15 minutes until the chicken is cooked through.

Serve with the turmeric rice and raita. This freezes well for up to a month.

PRAWN WONTONS WITH GREEN APPLE & CHILLI RELISH

This crowd-pleasing number is as you'd imagine – classic crunchy, prawny goodness with an exuberant sauce of apple and chilli. If you dare use the whole green chilli, then chill the sauce – you get a lovely tempestuous play of hot wontons and cool but spicy sauce on the palate. Err on the side of frying the wontons for a minute more than you'd expect to, and the skins will stay crisp for a lot longer. Also, any leftover sauce is great for dipping corn chips into.

30 wonton wrappers

2 litres rice bran OR sunflower oil, for deep-frying

GREEN APPLE & CHILLI RELISH

1 large green apple, unpeeled & cored OR 2 kiwifruit, peeled

1 long green chilli, roughly sliced, or to taste

3 tablespoons white vinegar

2 garlic cloves, peeled

1 tablespoon caster sugar

1 tablespoon fish sauce OR 1 teaspoon salt

¼ tightly packed cup roughly chopped coriander leaves (optional)

PRAWN FILLING

250 g prawn meat, roughly chopped*

1 tablespoon finely chopped ginger

2 spring onions, finely chopped

2 tablespoons Shaoxing rice wine

¾ teaspoon soy sauce

½ teaspoon sugar

1 teaspoon sesame oil

Good couple of pinches of white pepper

2 teaspoons wheaten cornflour

FEEDS 4 AS AN APPETISER

DF

To make the green apple and chilli relish, blitz all the ingredients in a food processor or blender until smooth. Taste to see if the seasoning needs to be tweaked with more vinegar, sugar, fish sauce or salt. Cover with cling wrap pressed directly onto the surface of the relish and chill until needed to prevent discolouration.

To make the prawn filling, mix all the ingredients together in a bowl.

Place a small teaspoon of the prawn filling in the middle of a wonton wrapper, then fold in half into a triangle. Seal the edges with a little bit of water, making sure to press out any air pockets**. Place the wonton on a plate or baking tray and repeat with the remaining wrappers and filling.

Meanwhile, heat the deep-frying oil in a medium saucepan or wok over medium–high heat. To check if the oil is ready, rest the tips of a pair of wooden chopsticks on the bottom of the pan and if a steady flurry of bubble rises to the top, it's ready. If unsure, test to see if a wonton cooks in about 15 seconds – any less and the oil might be too hot. Fill the surface of the oil with a single layer of wontons and fry until golden and crisp. Transfer the cooked wontons to a paper towel–lined colander or sieve. Repeat until all the wontons are fried.

Serve the wontons hot with the cool and spicy apple and chilli relish.

*You can chop the prawn meat by hand or pulse in a food processor.

**You can fry them like this (the simplest) or if you like the gold ingot shape I've used, simply pull the opposite pointy ends of the wonton to overlap each other slightly and press to seal in place.

WHITE FISH WITH MISO BEURRE BLANC, SALMON ROE & GREEN SALAD

When I haven't eaten beurre blanc for a while, I forget how it exemplifies French technique and exquisite balance at the gentle end of the spectrum. Vegos, you can omit the salmon roe and replace the pipis and fish with king oyster or enoki mushrooms.

A couple of handfuls of pipis (cockles)

2 x 200 g snapper fillets OR any white fish OR 300 g king oyster mushrooms, sliced into 2 cm thick medallions OR 300 g bunch of enoki mushrooms*

Olive oil

MISO BEURRE BLANC

3 tablespoons white wine vinegar

3 tablespoons white wine

2 small eschalots OR ½ small red onion, finely chopped

180 g chilled unsalted butter, diced into 2 cm pieces

1 teaspoon shiro (white) miso

2 tablespoons lemon juice

Salt & white pepper

2 tablespoons salmon roe

GREEN SALAD

2 heaped teaspoons dijon mustard

3 tablespoons lemon juice OR white wine vinegar

2½ tablespoons olive oil

Salt & freshly ground black pepper

1 oak leaf lettuce, leaves rinsed & torn into bite-sized pieces

FEEDS 2

GF / VO

To make the miso beurre blanc, combine the vinegar, white wine and shallot or onion in a small saucepan over medium–low heat, bring to a simmer and cook until reduced to roughly 2 tablespoons of liquid. Strain the liquid through a sieve into a bowl, pressing the shallot to remove as much liquid as possible. Return the liquid to the saucepan over low heat. Add one cube of butter at a time, whisking well and waiting for it to melt completely between additions. Don't rush this or the sauce will split. Once all the butter is added, whisk in the miso and lemon juice. Taste, then season carefully with salt and white pepper. Just before serving, fold in the salmon roe.

To cook the pipis, place them in a small saucepan with about 3 cm of boiling water and allow them to steam until opened. Leave covered until needed.

Allow the fish to come to room temperature (about 10 minutes). Season both sides with salt and pepper. Heat a dash of olive oil in a non-stick frying pan over medium–high heat. Cook the fish fillets on both sides until cooked through – if I were to describe how to achieve perfect 'doneness' here, it would take half a page, so I implore you to do what I did when I once had no idea, which is to pay the fish a lot of attention, and do things like prod or insert a paring knife at its thickest part for a sneaky peek, then make a judgement call. Just remember that the residual heat will keep cooking the fish while resting, so account for this. Hopefully you have a bit of caramelisation on the flesh. Skinless fillets are particularly hard to keep intact so don't stress if it's not picture-perfect – the beurre blanc will cover a myriad of sins!

If using mushrooms, the trick to cooking big chunks like this is to employ the dumpling steam-fry method. Steam them, covered, in about 1 cm of water with oil or butter, until they're cooked through. Remove the lid and allow the water to evaporate, leaving the fat behind to finish caramelising.

For the green salad, combine the dijon mustard, lemon juice or vinegar, olive oil and salt and pepper in a clean glass jar and shake until mixed well. Pour over the lettuce at the very last minute and toss gently with clean hands.

Place the cooked fish or mushrooms on serving plates, arrange the cooked pipis around them, then pour the beurre blanc over to coat well. Serve immediately with the salad in the middle of the table to share.

*If using enoki, trim the ends and halve the entire bunch lengthways, keeping the clusters intact so you can easily cook them like steaks.

SALTY

DEFO EURO

Classics

CAVATELLI WITH ANCHOVY BUTTER & FRESH TOMATO

If you don't count melting butter as cooking, this is another of my god-daughter Cassie Lee's supremely clever pasta sauces that requires no cooking. You could heat up the leftover Bagna Cauda from page 171 in the microwave or on the stove, which would be perfect for the job, otherwise this anchovy and garlic paste is even simpler. As with many recipes in this book, the amounts are really about what excites your palate – trust yourself and just go for it.

½ x quantity Handmade Semolina Cavatelli (page 135) OR 200 g store-bought pasta

50–100 g unsalted butter, melted

A decent couple of glugs of olive oil

250 g punnet of cherry tomatoes, diced into 1 cm pieces

Handful of fresh basil leaves, torn

½ teaspoon dried chilli flakes (optional)

Freshly ground black pepper

Finely grated lemon zest (optional)

ANCHOVY & GARLIC PASTE

12–15 anchovy fillets (up to you how intense you like it)

1 garlic clove, peeled

1 long red chilli (optional)

FEEDS 2

To make the anchovy and garlic paste, use a mortar and pestle to pound and grind the anchovy fillets, garlic and chilli (if using) until well combined.

Cook the cavatelli following the instructions on page 135, reserving about 125 ml (½ cup) of the pasta cooking water.

Transfer the pasta to a large non-stick frying pan. Add the prepared paste, the melted butter and a few tablespoons of the reserved pasta cooking water and toss or fold everything together over medium heat until the sauce turns glossy and coats the pasta well.

Divide the pasta into bowls, then top with the fresh tomato, basil and chilli flakes (if using). Before serving, season with pepper and a fine grating of lemon zest, if using.

ROASTED CAULI, GRUYERE SAUCE, HAZELNUTS, CRISPY KALE & POACHIES

I used to serve this at Jamface as a brunch item, but it makes for such a lovely cold-weather vegetarian dinner, served with some rustic bread to mop up every skerrick of gruyere sauce. It's all here – tender, charred cauliflower and buttery poached eggs, covered in a blanket of luxurious sauce, crunchy hazelnuts, then finished with crispy kale.

4–6 kale leaves, stripped from the stem, leaves torn into 5 cm pieces

Olive oil

½ large cauliflower, cut into bite-sized florets

Salt & freshly ground black pepper

4–8 poached eggs (follow the method on page 180)

65 g roasted hazelnuts, roughly chopped

2 tablespoons finely sliced chives

GRUYERE SAUCE

30 g butter

20 g flour

300 ml hot milk

2½ tablespoons cream

60 g (½ cup) grated gruyere

1 garlic clove, peeled & bashed to split (optional)

Pinch of freshly grated nutmeg

Salt & white pepper

FEEDS 4

V

Preheat the oven to 100°C fan-forced and line two baking trays with baking paper.

To make the crispy kale, toss the leaves with a few decent glugs of olive oil. Spread them in a single layer on one of the trays and roast for about 20 minutes or until completely crisp. Set aside until needed.

Increase the oven temperature to 250°C fan-forced.

Place the cauliflower in a bowl and toss with a few decent glugs of olive oil. Arrange in a single layer on the second tray and roast for 10–15 minutes or until tender and the edges are mildly charred.

To make the gruyere sauce, combine the butter and flour in a medium non-stick saucepan and stir over medium heat until foaming and golden. Add the milk, cream, gruyere and garlic (if using) and whisk until thickened and smooth. Taste and add nutmeg, salt and pepper.

Divide the cauli among serving plates, then top with the eggs, gruyere sauce, hazelnuts, chives and crispy kale and serve immediately.

T-BONE STEAK WITH BAGNA CAUDA & CHARRED FENNEL

I'm not going to lie. I often give myself a pat on the back for discovering this heavenly combination because it's such a tidy unit of comfort and class, luxurious yet restrained. My love for bagna cauda runs so deep I've even been asked to speak about it on Italian radio, where I found out it's a thing I have in common with Pope Francis! Traditionally bagna cauda is eaten with crudités, but while fossicking around in the fridge for steak condiments, I spotted the revelatory tub of leftover bagna cauda. I believe it spoke to me, saying, 'If you don't douse my creamy, anchovy godliness over your steak, your life will be incomplete.'

2 x T-bone steaks (aged if possible)

Olive oil

Salt & freshly ground black pepper

1 large fennel bulb, bottom & tips trimmed, halved lengthways & cut into 8 wedges

Handful of flat-leaf parsley leaves, roughly chopped

BAGNA CAUDA

12 garlic cloves, peeled

Milk

20 anchovy fillets

200 g unsalted butter

170 ml (⅔ cup) olive oil

80 ml (⅓ cup) cream

FEEDS 2

GF

To make the bagna cauda, place the garlic in a saucepan over medium–low heat and add just enough milk to cover the cloves. Add the anchovy fillets and simmer until the garlic is soft enough to be easily mashed with a fork. Add the remaining ingredients and blitz with a stick blender until smooth. If it splits on resting, warm it gently over low heat while whisking until re-emulsified. This keeps very well in an airtight container in the fridge for up to 2 weeks, or in the freezer for up to 2 months.

Allow the steaks to come to room temperature before cooking. Massage them with plenty of olive oil, then season generously on both sides with salt and pepper.

In a medium bowl, toss the fennel wedges in a few good glugs of olive oil, then season well with salt and pepper.

Heat a cast-iron chargrill pan until smoking. Cook the fennel wedges on both sides until distinct bar marks appear but a good deal of crunch is retained – the trick is to leave them alone and only turn once! Transfer them to a plate and cover with foil to keep warm.

Cook the steaks to your preferred doneness, remembering to cook the sides especially if there's a decent amount of fat. Like cooking any protein, this is all about practice, prodding and maybe inserting the tip of a knife closest to the bone to check. An important point, though, is to rest the steak for half the time you've cooked it, so the juices and tenderness are retained.

Serve the steak with the fennel on the side. Go nuts with the bagna cauda (which also goes incredibly well with lamb chopperoos), then top with the chopped parsley.

'I lose my nerve daily. Every time I sit in front of an easel I'm anxious that my hands might not work. Whenever I haven't cooked something in a while I wonder if I've forgotten how. When I sit in front of a keyboard, I'm worried I won't be able to find the words. It's a hundred cups of procrastination tea before an act of faith every day.'

marigolds

Multix®
CONTENTS   DATE
Straw Flowers
or
Paper Daisy

CONTENTS
Multix®
Pink Flower
DATE

red daisy ground cover

MIX SEEDS

Mango Seeds

Let your flowers go to seed, then
collect them for swapping and
next-season planting.

ZEN'S CREAMY ZUCCHINI & ANCHO PASTA SAUCE

This is another fiendishly simple pasta sauce, first introduced to me by my dear friend Zen. He doesn't use chilli in his version, but I like how it cuts through the cream. If you're not doing carbs this would make a perfectly good bed of sauce for a piece of white protein to sit on.

10–12 anchovy fillets

2–3 garlic cloves, crushed or finely chopped

½ teaspoon dried chilli flakes, or to taste

25 g butter

Decent glug of olive oil

2 zucchini, coarsely grated

200 ml cream OR milk

Finely grated zest of ½ lemon

Salt & freshly ground black pepper

1 x quantity Handmade Semolina Cavatelli (page 135)

3 tablespoons roughly chopped flat-leaf parsley leaves

Freshly grated parmesan OR pecorino, to serve

FEEDS 3–4

Combine the anchovy fillets, garlic, chilli flakes, butter and olive oil in a medium non-stick frying pan over medium heat and cook until the anchovy fillets are dissolved. Add the zucchini and sauté for about 10 seconds, then add the cream (or milk if you prefer it less rich) and lemon zest. Season carefully as the anchovies are already salty.

Cook the cavatelli following the instructions on page 135, then drain and add to the sauce. Toss and fold until the sauce thickens and coats the pasta evenly. Top with the parsley and serve with the parmesan or pecorino in the middle of the table for diners to help themselves.

PRAWN & ASPARAGUS RISOTTO WITH BURNT SAGE BUTTER

This dish is a stunner and its strength totally lies in making prawn stock from the shells, so you get that deep bisque-y deliciousness infused into the rice. I'd prefer not to upset all the Italians in my life, so no cheese with seafood, but a microplaning of lemon zest instead. Also, a quantity tip for future reference – it's 100 g rice per person when making risotto.

3 tablespoons olive oil

½ onion, diced into 5 mm pieces

Salt & freshly ground black pepper

200 g arborio OR carnaroli rice

100 ml white wine

50 g butter

10–12 sage leaves

400 g prawns, peeled, deveined & cut into 1 cm chunks (heads & shells reserved for stock)

6 fat asparagus spears, ends snapped off* & discarded, stalks cut into 1 cm pieces OR 70 g (½ cup) frozen peas

2 tablespoons lemon juice, or to taste

PRAWN STOCK

Reserved prawn heads & shells (see above)

1 litre (4 cups) water

½ small fennel bulb OR ½ celery stalk, sliced

½ medium onion, sliced

½ medium carrot, peeled & sliced

1–2 parsley stalks, chopped

Salt, to taste

TO SERVE

Finely grated lemon zest

Flat-leaf parsley leaves (optional)

FEEDS 2

GF

To make the prawn stock, combine all the ingredients in a medium saucepan and simmer for 10 minutes. Remove from the heat and allow the ingredients to steep while you prep the risotto. When ready to use, strain the stock and return it to the saucepan, covered, on the lowest simmer possible. Discard the shells and vegetables. Taste and season the stock.

To make the risotto, combine the olive oil and onion in a heavy-based saucepan over medium heat. Sauté with a good pinch of salt until the onion is soft and translucent but not coloured. Stir in the rice until all the grains are coated in the oil, then add a few ladles of the prawn stock and the wine. Simmer until most of the liquid is absorbed, then add more ladles of stock. Repeat until the rice is al dente – that is, mostly tender except for a speck of residual crunch at the centre. Taste and season if needed.

Melt the butter in a medium non-stick frying pan over medium–high heat and allow it to go brown. Immediately add the sage leaves (watch out, these spit a little), then the prawn and asparagus or peas. It should only take a matter of seconds for the prawn and asparagus or peas to cook perfectly. Add the lemon juice but once again be aware of spitting. Taste and season.

Spoon the risotto onto plates, then, using the ladle, make an indent in the centre of the pools of rice and fill with the prawn, asparagus or peas and burnt butter. Garnish with a few crispy sage leaves, a microplaning of lemon zest and a light sprinkling of parsley if you like.

*To snap the end off asparagus, hold a spear about halfway down with your non-dominant hand and bend it about 4 cm in from the cut end with your other hand, until it snaps. This will get rid of whatever is fibrous.

JOÉLLE'S OEUFS EN MEURETTE

You can eat this for breakfast, lunch or dinner. The first time I watched this dish being made was unpredictable from beginning to end. It's not the prettiest dish, but putting it into context will help you imagine the flavours and textures. Joélle (my bestie Sarah's mum) explained that the origins of oeufs en meurette come from cooking potatoes and poaching eggs in leftover boeuf bourguignon sauce. This is her vegetarian version using mushrooms instead of beef, which do the job with stunning aplomb. Cooking the eggs in the bourguignon sauce the traditional way will taste better, but the wine will stain them grey and it's a little messier to control their doneness and shape than if you cook them in water, so you choose.

50 g butter

Dash of olive oil

12 sprigs of thyme

500 ml (2 cups) red wine

250 ml (1 cup) vegetable OR chicken stock

2 potatoes (whatever your fave variety is), peeled & diced into 2 cm pieces

½ baguette, finely sliced diagonally

125 g butter, melted

1 garlic clove, peeled & halved

8 fresh* large eggs

2 tablespoons white vinegar

3 tablespoons roughly chopped flat-leaf parsley leaves

Salt & freshly ground black pepper

MIRÉPOIX

1 large onion, peeled & quartered

1 carrot, peeled & cut into 4–5 chunks

1 celery stalk, cut into 4–5 chunks

400 g white OR Swiss brown mushrooms

BEURRE MANIÉ

50 g softened butter

50 g (⅓ cup) plain flour

FEEDS 4

VO

To make the mirépoix, combine the onion, carrot, celery and mushrooms in a food processor and blitz to a fine-ish 5 mm chop. If you don't have a food processor, finely chop these guys by hand.

Partially melt the butter with the olive oil in a saucepan over medium heat, then add the mirépoix and thyme. Sauté until the aromatics are soft and fragrant but not coloured. Add the red wine and stock and allow to simmer very gently, uncovered, for 15–20 minutes or until reduced by one-third.

Pass the mixture through a muslin-lined sieve, and wring as much of the liquid out as possible – use your guns, peeps! Discard the solids, then return the liquid to the saucepan and bring to a simmer.

Meanwhile, make the beurre manié by mashing the softened butter and flour together in a bowl, or on a plate, until you have a smooth paste. Whisk enough of this into the simmering sauce until thickened slightly, like soup. Taste, then season.

Steam the potato until tender.

Preheat the oven to 160°C fan-forced and line a baking tray with baking paper.

Brush all the baguette slices generously with the melted butter, then rub lightly with the garlic. Toast on the baking tray in the oven for about 10 minutes or until dark golden and crisp all the way through.

Poach the eggs following the instructions on page 180.

You can serve this all hot on a large platter, but I like to divide it into individual bowls or cocottes. Layer each with one-quarter of the potato, then two eggs. Season before ladling on one-quarter of the sauce and garnishing with parsley. Place the croutons on side plates and serve hot.

*Fresh eggs hold together better when poaching. Otherwise the whites scatter into a hundred threads and you lose half of it to the poaching water. BUT, if it happens, don't sweat it.

DEFO EURO

ASPARAGUS, HOLLANDAISE, EGGS & HAM

I will happily have this for any meal of the day. It's flavour and French technique personified, only improved if you have the good fortune to come across white asparagus, which ups the luxury factor by another half. Did you know the way they make the asparagus stay pearlescent is to grow it in the dark and keep mounding earth over it as it shoots? The light-deprivation is what prevents the chlorophyll from developing.

8 fresh* large eggs

2 tablespoons white vinegar

4 bunches of asparagus, ends snapped off**

Olive oil

Salt & freshly ground black pepper

Butter

8 slices of double-smoked ham

HOLLANDAISE

3 egg yolks

1–2 tablespoons lemon juice

1 teaspoon dijon mustard

125 g unsalted butter, melted

Salt, to taste

Pinch of freshly ground white OR cayenne pepper

FEEDS 4

VO (OMIT HAM)

Preheat the oven to 180°C fan-forced. Line a baking tray with baking paper.

To poach the eggs, have a large bowl of cool water on standby. Begin by filling a medium saucepan with water and the vinegar. Bring to a simmer. Swirl the outer edge of the water with a wooden spoon to create a whirlpool. Quickly crack and drop the eggs in one by one (putting them in a teacup first is a good idea just in case the yolks burst). If the whirlpool dissipates, just stir again. You can drop as many eggs as you like into the whirlpool. Curiously, they will stay separate. Keep an eye on the eggs, they should take about 5 minutes for a runny centre but, I'm not going to lie, this takes practice. You just have to keep fishing the individual eggs out with a slotted spoon and go for a poke and fondle for the right 'doneness'. When you trust they are right (firm whites with a nicely wobbly yolk), slide them gently into the bowl of cool water so they stop cooking. Turn off the heat, but leave the pan on the stove for making the hollandaise.

Next, arrange the asparagus in a single layer on the prepared tray. Drizzle with a little olive oil, then season lightly with salt and pepper. Pop in the oven for about 5 minutes – you want tender spears but with a residual crunch.

At the same-ish time, I would whizz a bit of butter over the base of a large non-stick frying pan over high heat, then give all the ham a bit of a scrunch and cram it all in the pan. I like doing this so the folds get a bit of caramelisation but most of it remains succulent. Set aside.

Meanwhile, to make the hollandaise, whisk the yolks, just 1 tablespoon of the lemon juice to begin with and the mustard in a medium heatproof bowl sitting over the egg-poaching saucepan comfortably, with the heat off. You can melt the butter using the microwave or stove, but it should be hot. Drizzle in one-quarter of the melted butter and whisk enthusiastically. Repeat until all the butter is used up. The sauce should be beautiful and thick. Taste and season with salt and white or cayenne pepper and more lemon juice if you like. If you split the sauce, add a tablespoon of hot water and another egg yolk, then blitz the crap out of it with a stick blender – it always does the trick!

Just before serving, bring the poaching water back to a simmer, turn the heat off, then gently slide in the eggs, one at time. Let the eggs warm up for about 5 minutes.

I've plated this a bit fancy in the pic, but to serve I usually just layer in the following order: asparagus, eggs, then ham (to hide the eggs if they look a disgrace, but also because the folds in the ham will catch more hollandaise sauce, which you pour over top). Good luck making it all hot – I'm terrible at it but no one ever cares because it's so delicious!

*See page 178 for why freshness is important.

**See page 177 for how to do this.

DEFO EURO

With grief always comes renewal.
Losing a job, a loved one, failing at something.
It's these moments that teach you the most.
It's when you feel you've lost everything that
life gives you a chance at re-invention.

'Want a charming knife block that costs near to nothing? Fill a large vintage jug with rice. You can cram as many knives as you can fit in the mouth of the jug and the rice is gentle on the blades!'

JERUSALEM ARTICHOKE VELOUTÉ WITH TRUFFLE OIL

I always 'ave a larf when I see Jerusalem artichokes because it reminds me of walking past them in Season 1 of *MasterChef* and thinking 'weird ginger'. We were proper humble home cooks back then! But let's discuss the flavour – sweet, subtly earthy and, honestly, one of the most ethereal flavours I've ever tasted. When I used to do Crunch Club at Jamface, it was one of the few dishes that always caused a no-joke bowl-licking situation! As for the truffle oil, a lot of food snobs will crap all over it, but I really despise snobbery and if you don't have the means, this is as close as you'll get to that curious nugget of fungus, also referred to as 'black gold', so I say, douse away!

1 large onion, finely chopped

1–2 garlic cloves, crushed or finely chopped

25 g unsalted butter

Dash of olive oil

Salt & white pepper

1 litre (4 cups) chicken OR vegetable stock, plus extra if needed (water or milk is also fine)

1 kg Jerusalem artichokes, scrubbed well & finely sliced

125 ml (½ cup) thickened cream

1 tablespoon finely sliced chives

1 tablespoon truffle oil (white if possible)

VELOUTÉ

50 g unsalted butter

2 tablespoons plain flour

250 ml (1 cup) milk

FEEDS 4

VO

To make the velouté, melt the butter with the flour in a medium saucepan over medium heat and stir until it foams. Add the milk and whisk until smooth. Set aside.

Combine the onion, garlic, butter and olive oil in a large saucepan and cook over medium heat with a generous pinch of salt (so the aromatics don't brown too quickly) until soft and translucent. Add the stock and Jerusalem artichoke and simmer until soft.

Blitz the artichoke mixture in a blender in small batches until smooth, return it to the pan, then whisk in the velouté until combined. Add more stock, water or milk until it reaches your preferred viscosity, then whisk in the cream. Taste and season with salt and pepper.

Serve hot, topped with the chives and finished with a drizzle of truffle oil.

SUMMER PEA & MINT RISOTTO

This has become my favourite summer risotto as it's so light and fresh but also convenient, because I always have peas in the freezer and mint running rampant in the garden in the warmer months. Another plus is that it takes so little time to whip up. Feel free to replace the onion with a leek, or the peas with spinach. Err on the side of not over-blitzing your peas and mint or they will oxidise and you will lose that vibrant green and also dull the flavour. If you want to spoil yourself, a dollop of créme fraîche and a spoonful of salmon roe to finish would be pretty delightful.

1 litre (4 cups) cool chicken OR vegetable stock (you can sub out 250 ml (1 cup) of this for milk for added richness)

1 onion, diced into 5 mm pieces

2–3 tablespoons olive oil

Salt

300 g (1⅓ cups) arborio rice

230 g (1¾ cups) frozen baby peas

Handful of mint leaves

50 g butter

30 g finely grated parmesan, or to taste

FEEDS 2–3

GF / VO

Reserve 125 ml (½ cup) of the cool stock before bringing the rest to the boil. Turn the heat off and cover until needed.

Combine the onion and olive oil in a medium saucepan over medium heat with a pinch of salt and cook until the onion is soft and translucent. Stir in the rice, then one-third of the stock. Bring to a simmer, then stir to make sure the bottom isn't catching.

Meanwhile, in a jug use a stick blender to puree 130 g (1 cup) of the peas and the mint with the reserved cool stock (but water is also fine). Set aside.

Keep adding 125 ml (½ cup) of stock to the rice at a time, stirring and allowing it to absorb, until the risotto reaches a porridgy consistency and the rice is cooked but with a residual crunch at the centre. Turn the heat off and fold the butter and parmesan through until melted. Fold in the pea and mint puree and the remaining whole peas. Taste, season and serve immediately.

SALTY

WANDERLUST

No passport required

SREYMOM'S CAMBODIAN FISH AMOK
WITH COCONUT RICE & ASIAN SLAW

Sreymom worked as a manager at Jamface and is one of the most resilient, brave, stubborn, capable women I know. She opened Little Khmer Kitchen to showcase Cambodian food and this is one of many of my favourite dishes served there. I'm thrilled she agreed to share this recipe because it's honestly one of the most delicious things you'll ever taste. Something I love about this recipe is that I grew up with the Malaysian version of it, called otak otak, and it's a reminder of how wonderfully food can reveal cultural stories of shared lands, ideas and genetics.

KHMER KROEUNG SPICE PASTE

2 makrut* lime leaves, centre vein sliced away, tender parts sliced paper-thin

1 long red chilli, roughly sliced

1 bird's eye chilli, roughly sliced

20 g belachan (shrimp paste; found in the Asian section of supermarkets or at Asian grocers; optional)

2 medium shallots OR ½ red onion, peeled & quartered

30 g galangal, finely sliced

30 g fresh turmeric, roughly sliced OR 2–3 teaspoons ground turmeric

3 garlic cloves, peeled

3–4 stalks of lemongrass, pale parts only, finely sliced

3 tablespoons coconut milk

FISH AMOK

500 g white fish fillets OR prawn meat, cut into 2 cm pieces

125 ml (½ cup) Khmer Kroeung Spice Paste (see above)

2 eggs, lightly whisked

125 ml (½ cup) coconut milk

1 tablespoon fish sauce

1 tablespoon sugar

COCONUT RICE TOPPING

150 ml coconut cream

½ teaspoon sugar

2–3 teaspoons rice flour

¼ teaspoon salt, or to taste

1 cm piece of ginger, lightly pounded to split & no more

Handful of fried shallots

550 g (3 cups) cooked jasmine rice**

SALAD DRESSING

3 tablespoons fish sauce

3 tablespoons rice vinegar OR white vinegar

2 tablespoons sugar

2 garlic cloves, finely chopped

1 bird's eye chilli, finely sliced

2 tablespoons lime OR lemon juice

100 ml coconut milk

ASIAN SLAW

¼ red OR white cabbage, finely sliced

2 carrots, peeled & coarsely grated

6 spring onions, finely sliced

100 g young coconut flesh (found in the freezer section of Asian grocers)

1 small red capsicum, quartered lengthways & finely sliced

Handful of Vietnamese mint leaves (laksa leaves)

Handful of mint leaves

Handful of coriander leaves, roughly chopped

70 g (½ cup) roughly chopped roasted peanuts

BANANA LEAF BASKETS

8 x 22 cm square sheets of banana leaves (check for splits)

16 toothpicks

FEEDS 4

GF / DF

*As the word kaffir is offensive in some cultures, I've chosen to use its alternative name.

**See page 90 for how to cook rice by the absorption method.

SREYMOM'S CAMBODIAN FISH AMOK
WITH COCONUT RICE & ASIAN SLAW (CONT.)

To make the khmer kroeung spice paste, combine all the ingredients in a blender and pulse until smooth. Extra paste can be frozen for up to 2 months.

To make the fish amok, place the fish and khmer kroeung paste in a bowl, mix well and allow to marinate for 2 hours if possible or 10 minutes minimum.

To make the coconut rice topping, whisk together the coconut cream, sugar, rice flour and salt in a small saucepan over medium heat until combined. Add the ginger and simmer until thickened, then remove from the heat and set aside.

To make the salad dressing, shake all the ingredients in a clean glass jar until combined.

Mix enough dressing with all the Asian slaw ingredients, except the peanuts, to taste – garnish with the peanuts just before serving. Extra dressing can be kept in a jar in the fridge for up to 4 days.

To prepare the banana leaf baskets, follow the diagram below. If you are using fresh banana leaves, they must be blanched in boiling water to soften first. If using frozen, they will already be soft.

When you are ready to cook, whisk together the remaining fish amok ingredients in a small bowl. Add this to the marinated fish, then divide the mixture among the four banana leaf baskets. Steam in a bamboo or stainless steel steaming basket for 15 minutes or until the fish is cooked through.

Place one fish amok basket on each serving plate with some salad. Add a serve of rice to each plate and spoon over 2 tablespoons of the coconut rice topping. Finish with a sprinkle of fried shallots and serve immediately.

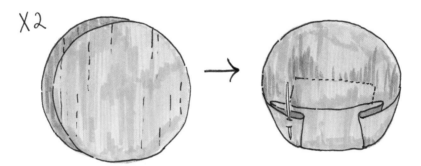

Use a double layer of banana leaves. Trace around a plate that's roughly 20 cm in diameter.

Make a pleat at four even intervals of the circle and secure with toothpicks.

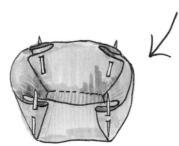

As I get older, I'm learning I don't always have to shimmy, that I'm good enough just standing still.

THAI-STYLE SAGO DUMPLINGS WITH SWEET PEPPER PORK IN LETTUCE CUPS

This is a bastardised version (but, I feel, just as delicious) of the traditional Thai saku sai mu, which is a sago dumpling stuffed with pork. I wanted so badly to make them for our Jamface Crunch Club Friday night dinners, but holy moly they're a sticky, fiddly affair. So the next best thing was to deconstruct the elements into more easily made components. Imagine gorgeously squidgy cubes of sago coated in crispy garlic oil; sweet, salty, peppery pork wrapped in crisp, cool lettuce leaves; all topped with refreshing sprigs of coriander and small bursts of chilli all in a single mouthful – a delightful play of texture and flavour. For vegos and vegans, swap out the fish sauce for soy, then double the amount of peanuts to replace the pork.

2–3 tablespoons vegetable OR peanut oil

1 onion, diced into 5 mm pieces

100 g reasonably fatty coarse pork mince

70 g (½ cup) roasted peanuts, roughly chopped

1 tablespoon fish sauce

2–3 tablespoons sugar

1 teaspoon freshly ground black pepper

GARLIC OIL

3 garlic cloves, crushed

3 tablespoons vegetable oil

SAGO DUMPLINGS

Olive oil spray

90 g (½ cup) sago (tapioca) pearls, soaked in cool water for about 1 hour

BITS & PIECES

2–3 gem OR baby cos lettuces (iceberg is also great), leaves separated, rinsed & drained

Small bunch of coriander

½ long red chilli, finely sliced

FEEDS 4 AS AN APPETISER

GF / DF / VGO

To make the garlic oil, combine the garlic and vegetable oil in a small saucepan over medium heat and cook until the garlic turns a pale golden colour. Stir and remove from the heat immediately. Cool the oil in a bowl.

To make the dumplings, thoroughly spray the base and side of a 22 cm round heatproof dish with olive oil spray. Drain the sago in a sieve, pressing gently to release any excess moisture. Spread the sago evenly over the prepared dish, then press the surface slightly so it is nice and flat. Place the dish on a trivet or in a bamboo steamer to steam on the highest heat until the sago is translucent. Immediately tip it upside down onto a chopping board that has been well sprayed with olive oil. With a wet knife, slice the sago into 2 cm cubes. It's a sticky affair, so wet your hands as you separate the cubes, then toss them well in the garlic oil to keep them separated.

To cook the pork, combine the vegetable or peanut oil and onion in a medium non-stick frying pan over medium–high heat and cook until the onion is soft and caramelised. Add the pork mince and stir-fry until cooked through. Add the peanuts, fish sauce, sugar and pepper and cook until caramelised and no liquid remains.

To serve, place 8–10 cubes of the sago on a lettuce leaf, then add a couple of tablespoons of pork. Garnish with a few leaves of coriander and slices of chilli. Repeat until you run out of ingredients and serve on a large platter in the centre of the table for diners to help themselves.

FISH-FRAGRANT EGGPLANT & BASHED CUCUMBER SALAD

My globe-trotting, not-so-little-anymore goddaughter, Cassie Lee, cooked this classic Szechuanese beauty for me after time spent in China teaching English and learning to speak Mandarin, and it's become one of my favourite ways to celebrate eggplant. If you stir-fry the eggplant it will brown more randomly, but I like to give this part a lot of love and pan-fry every side of the batons. You'll get the most beautiful silken lengths of eggplant, consistently tender all the way through, and the cucumber salad will cool you down twofold – you can vent any personal frustrations through the bashing, but it also provides refreshing respite to the spicy, oily eggplant. This is equally lovely when served chilled.

CUCUMBER SALAD

1 continental cucumber, bashed with a rolling pin or pestle until split, then roughly sliced into bite-sized pieces

125 ml (½ cup) rice wine vinegar

55 g (¼ cup) caster sugar

2 tablespoons fish sauce

1 teaspoon sesame oil

1 bird's eye chilli, split in half lengthways

1 teaspoon toasted sesame seeds

¼ cup roughly chopped coriander leaves

SZECHUAN SAUCE

2 tablespoons doubanjiang (fermented chilli bean paste; found in the Asian section of supermarkets or at Asian grocers)

2 tablespoons light soy sauce OR tamari

2 tablespoons Chinkiang vinegar (found in the Asian section of supermarkets or at Asian grocers)

2 tablespoons Shaoxing rice wine

2 tablespoons water

1 tablespoon wheaten OR maize cornflour

2 teaspoons sugar

EGGPLANT

2 medium–large eggplants, cut into 5 x 2 x 2 cm batons

125 ml (½ cup) olive oil, plus extra if needed

3 garlic cloves, crushed

2 tablespoons finely shredded ginger

3 spring onions, finely sliced, plus extra to serve

Steamed rice, to serve

FEEDS 4

GFO / DF / VGO (REPLACE FISH SAUCE WITH SOY)

To make the cucumber salad, mix all the ingredients, except the sesame seeds and coriander, in a bowl, then cover and chill. After 10 minutes, give it another mix, then leave it in the fridge until needed. Just before serving, drain the cucumbers, then mix in the sesame seeds and coriander.

Place all the Szechuan sauce ingredients in a bowl and mix well.

In a large non-stick frying pan over high heat, stir-fry the eggplant in two or three batches with about 2 tablespoons of olive oil per batch, or fry more fastidiously by turning the pieces to brown every side. You might need more oil than suggested as eggplants are very thirsty! Transfer the browned eggplant to a plate.

Using the same frying pan, combine 2 tablespoons of the olive oil with the garlic, ginger and spring onion and sauté until just starting to turn golden. Return the eggplant to the frying pan. Give the sauce ingredients a final stir before adding to the pan with the eggplant. When the sauce thickens, remove from the heat.

Sprinkle with some spring onion and serve hot with steamed rice and the cucumber salad.

'Don't try to defy the natural order of things because all that is meaningful and good JUST TAKES TIME, like a quality ferment! When we desire things outside of natural order, it can really bite us, like desiring the by-product of fame over love of craft. I've learnt that wanting something you haven't sacrificed for makes for a hollow journey. Blind ambition can have us steering doggedly towards the prize, ignoring that the path is always splitting and offering us opportunities to re-assess – is this really making me happy? Am I doing this coming from a place of authenticity or insecurity?'

fake ↘

AFGHAN-STYLE RICE WITH CAULIFLOWER OR CHICKEN

Afghan-style rice has become my favourite way to cook and eat basmati rice. The balance of flavours is wonderful – a subtle use of spice, lovely punctuations of sweetness from the carrots and currants, the crunch of roasted pistachios, then a hit of vibrancy from the yoghurt and coriander. But to die for are those super-light, beautifully separated grains of basmati that turn me into a rice-demolishing machine. You can omit the butter and yoghurt to make this vegan and dairy free.

125 ml (½ cup) olive oil*

3 onions, diced into 5 mm pieces

4 garlic cloves, finely chopped

1 tablespoon cumin seeds

1 teaspoon garam masala

1 teaspoon ground cardamom

Salt & freshly ground black pepper

400 g tin chopped tomatoes

½ head of cauliflower, cut into florets OR 8 chicken thigh fillets, halved

3 potatoes, peeled & diced into 2 cm pieces (optional)

500 g (2½ cups) basmati rice

250 ml (1 cup) chicken OR vegetable stock

20 saffron threads (optional)

CARROTS & CURRANTS

3 small–medium carrots, peeled & julienned

125 ml (½ cup) water

¾ cup currants OR sultanas

3 teaspoons sugar

TO SERVE

1 bunch of coriander, roughly chopped

70 g (½ cup) roasted shelled pistachios, roughly chopped

130 g (½ cup) Greek yoghurt (optional)

FEEDS 4–5

GF / DFO / V / VGO

To make the carrots and currants, combine all the ingredients in a small saucepan over medium–low heat. Stir and simmer, covered, for about 5 minutes or until all the liquid is evaporated – the carrot should be soft but not falling apart, and the currants or sultanas plump and juicy. Set aside.

Combine the oil (and butter if using), onion, garlic, cumin, garam masala, cardamom and 1 teaspoon of salt in a medium non-stick frying pan over medium–high heat. Cook until softened and slightly golden and the spices are fragrant. Remove one-third of the oil, spices and aromatic biz and set aside in a bowl. Add the tomato, cauli or chicken and potato (if using) to the pan, then season with salt and pepper. Cover and simmer for 20 minutes or until the potato (and chicken, if using) are cooked through. Taste and season or add more cardamom and garam masala if needed.

Soak the basmati rice in cool water for 5 minutes, then rinse and drain in a sieve. Heat the stock in a small saucepan on the stove until you see whisps of steam. Remove from the heat. Rub the saffron threads (if using) between your fingers to crush them a little while sprinkling them into the stock. Allow to steep until needed.

Bring a large saucepan of water to the boil, add the rice and cook until al dente or about 80 per cent cooked through. Drain immediately, then return to the pan. Next, add the reserved onion and garlic spice mixture to the stock and saffron mixture and bring to the boil. Add this to the rice, fold very briefly to combine, then cover as quickly as possible to trap the heat. Allow to steam for about 20 minutes.

To serve, place the cauliflower or chicken in a large bowl and garnish with coriander. Transfer the rice to a large shallow bowl, then sprinkle the carrot and currant mix and the pistachios on top. Place the yoghurt in a small bowl, if using. Arrange all the dishes in the centre of the table for everyone to help themselves.

*You can replace some of this with butter, which I love!

MINI ISRAELI-STYLE FEAST

There's something about the tactile nature of using your fingers – the picking, tearing and mopping – that makes eating so much more convivial. Fattoush is one of the best salads you'll ever taste but, if you don't want to go to the trouble, then freshly cut radishes, tomato and cucumber are terrific for providing crunch and cleansing. A couple of bits of advice I'd give for the dips? Season with your undivided attention, and make sure you add enough lemon juice because the acidity is what knits the elements together and makes it all dance on the palate. Feel your way through these. Like most of the recipes in this book, trust that whatever is delicious to you is right, so add, subtract, taste and season as you will.

FEEDS 5–6

V / VGO (OMIT YOGHURT IN FATTOUSH)

ISRAELI PITA

2 teaspoons dry yeast

1 teaspoon caster sugar

350 ml warm water

750 g white bread flour, plus extra for dusting

2 teaspoons olive oil

2 teaspoons salt

Mix the yeast, sugar and water in a bowl. Cover and rest for 10–15 minutes. Once you can see the surface is foamy, pour the mixture into the bowl of an electric stand mixer fitted with the dough hook attachment. Add the flour and olive oil and mix for 2 minutes on the lowest setting. Add the salt and mix for another minute or until smooth and pliable. Remove the dough from the bowl, brush olive oil all over the inside of the bowl, then return the dough to it. Cover the bowl with a wet tea towel and allow the dough to rise in a warm, draught-free spot until double its original volume.

Roll the dough into a sausage, then divide into 8–10 pieces and roll into balls. Place on a floured surface and cover with a damp tea towel. Roll the balls out on a floured surface until 1 cm thick. Place on floured trays, covered with a damp tea towel, and leave in a warm spot until doubled in size.

Meanwhile, preheat the oven to 190°C fan-forced.

Dust the pitas off before placing them directly on the oven racks. Bake for about 10 minutes – the desired result is for them to puff up into balls, then collapse into soft fluffy cushions dotted with a bit of colour. Place them in a tea towel–lined basket and cover with a double layer of tea towel. Over this, scrunch a generous size piece of foil. Serve warm with the dips and fattoush.

BABAGANOUSH

2 eggplants

1–2 heaped dessertspoons light tahini

1–3 garlic cloves, crushed, or to taste

Up to 80 ml (⅓ cup) lemon juice

Salt & freshly ground black pepper

Olive oil, for drizzling

2 tablespoons roughly chopped flat-leaf parsley leaves

2 tablespoons pomegranate seeds (optional)

Place a cast-iron chargrill pan* over high heat until smoking. Char the entire surface of the eggplant aggressively, rotating it only when the skin is blackened. Cool until comfortable to handle, then peel away the skin or scoop out the flesh and place in a medium bowl. If at this point you find some parts of the eggplant uncooked and hard to remove, simply microwave these for 1–2 minutes.

Add the tahini, garlic and most of the lemon juice to the eggplant and mix well. Taste, then season and balance with more garlic and the remaining lemon juice if needed. Spread into a circle on a plate, making a dimple in the middle for a drizzle of olive oil to pool into. Garnish with the parsley and pomegranate seeds (if using). Serve at room temperature.

*Of course, a barbecue will work but it takes a while to ramp up the heat. A naked gas flame works too, but this can create a bit of a mess if the juices start to seep from the eggplant as it cooks.

HUMMUS

400 g tin chickpeas, drained, liquid reserved

65 g (¼ cup) light tahini

3 tablespoons lemon juice, plus extra if needed

1–3 garlic cloves, crushed, or to taste

2 tablespoons olive oil, plus extra to serve

Salt

Sweet paprika OR sumac, to serve

Blitz all the hummus ingredients except for the reserved chickpea liquid in a food processor until smooth. Add the reserved chickpea liquid, 1 tablespoon at a time, blitzing well between each addition, until you have the desired consistency – I like mine loose because it's lighter. Taste and season, adding more lemon juice if needed. Spread into a circle on a plate, making a dimple in the middle for a drizzle of olive oil to pool into. Sprinkle with paprika or sumac. Serve at room temperature.

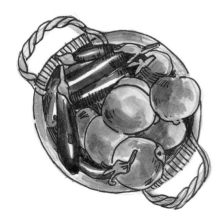

FATTOUSH

Any stale flatbread, torn into bite-sized pieces (about 2 cups)

1 continental cucumber, halved lengthways & sliced into 5 mm pieces

250 g punnet of cherry tomatoes, halved OR 2 large vine-ripened tomatoes, diced into 2 cm pieces

1 bunch of radishes (about 8)

90 g (¾ cup) finely sliced spring onion

½ packed cup mint leaves, roughly torn

1 packed cup flat-leaf parsley leaves

2 teaspoons dried mint

2 teaspoons sumac

DRESSING

3 tablespoons olive oil

130 g (½ cup) Greek yoghurt

3 tablespoons lemon juice OR cider OR white wine vinegar

1 garlic clove, crushed

2 tablespoons pomegranate molasses

Salt & freshly ground black pepper

Preheat the oven to 170°C fan-forced.

Spread the torn flatbread evenly on a baking tray and toast in the oven for about 15 minutes or until the edges are slightly charred.

Combine all the dressing ingredients in a clean glass jar and shake until smooth. Add salt and pepper to taste – always over-season a tad here as the liquid drawn out from the veg will dilute the intensity of the dressing.

Place all the salad ingredients and flatbread in a large salad bowl and toss gently. Shake the dressing well again and, just before serving, pour it over the salad. Toss gently until everything is well coated.

Clockwise from top left:
Israeli Pitas, Babaganoush,
Hummus and Fattoush.

GRILLED CHICKEN TORTILLAS WITH CHARRED CORN, KIWI SALSA & JALAPEÑO CREAM

You could just as easily layer all of this deliciousness in a sandwich, burger or taco – or just naked on a plate if you are carb-conscious. Pescatarians can sub out the chicken for prawns or fish, and vegos can chargrill thick pieces of zucchini or cauliflower. Also think about how you can repurpose the individual elements in other dishes. For instance, the kiwi salsa would go beautifully with something fried, and a dollop of the jalapeño cream served with a piece of pan-seared fish would work a treat!

600 g chicken tenderloins

Olive oil

Salt & freshly ground black pepper

4 sweetcorn cobs, husks removed

12 mini soft tortillas

300 g grated mozzarella

Lime wedges, to serve

KIWI SALSA

600 g kiwifruit, peeled & diced into 1 cm pieces

1 bunch of coriander, roughly chopped, including stalks

¼–½ red onion, diced into 5 mm pieces

Good dash of olive oil

Salt & freshly ground black pepper

JALAPEÑO CREAM

2 avocados, stones & skins removed

About 100 g (⅓–½ cup) pickled jalapeños, or to taste

125 g (½ cup) sour cream

120 g (1 cup) chopped spring onion

2 tablespoons lemon juice OR jalapeño brine from the jar

2 teaspoons caster sugar

Salt & freshly ground black pepper

FEEDS 4

VO

To make the kiwi salsa, place all the ingredients in a large bowl and fold gently to combine. Set aside.

To make the jalepeño cream, combine all the ingredients in a blender and pulse until smooth. Transfer to a bowl and set aside.

Heat a cast-iron chargrill pan over high heat until smoking. Brush the chicken with olive oil, then season on both sides. Cook until char marks appear and the chicken is cooked through. Transfer to a plate and cover with foil to keep warm.

To char the corn, simply brush with olive oil, season, then char slightly on all sides. To shave the corn, snap or cut the cobs in half. Stand a cob upright, making sure it is stable, then slice downwards with a sharp knife as close to the base of the kernels as possible. Repeat for the remaining corn, then transfer the kernels to a bowl.

Preheat the oven to 160°C fan-forced. Spread the tortillas out on a baking tray. Sprinkle with the mozzarella, then heat in the oven for about 6 minutes or until the mozzarella is melted and the tortillas are warmed through.

Place all the elements in the middle of the table for everyone to build their own tortillas.

SCANDI-STYLE
SMOKED SALMON, POTATO
& BOILED EGG SALAD

When I opened my cafe, I didn't want to serve bacon and eggs. I wanted a menu inspired by the exciting flavours of different landscapes and sensibilities. And after a trip to Sweden I came up with this. It has all the Scandi imperatives covered; with cured salmon, dill, eggs, potatoes and sour cream, it's rich, clean and hearty all at once and makes a perfect brunch dish.

2–3 kipfler potatoes, peeled & diced into 2 cm pieces

3–4 large eggs

Good pinch of bicarbonate of soda (for easier peeling)

4–6 slices of smoked salmon

2 radishes, finely sliced

A few dill leaves, for garnish

DILL DRESSING

1 tablespoon finely chopped dill fronds

3 polskie ogórki gherkins, diced into 5 mm pieces, plus 1 tablespoon brine from the jar

2 tablespoons finely chopped red onion

2 tablespoons capers, plus 1 tablespoon brine from the jar

1 teaspoon caster sugar

2 tablespoons olive oil

Finely grated zest & juice of ½ lemon

Salt & freshly ground black pepper

SOUR CREAM SAUCE

100 g sour cream

2 teaspoons horseradish, or to taste

1 teaspoon caster sugar

⅛ teaspoon salt, or to taste

FEEDS 2

GF

Boil the potatoes in salted water until tender. Drain and cool before using.

Place the eggs and bicarbonate of soda in a pan of cold water and bring to the boil. Turn the heat off and cover for 6 minutes for jammy yolks, or about double the time for hard yolks. Immediately plunge the eggs into plenty of cold water, then peel and halve when the eggs are completely cooled.

Mix the dill dressing ingredients together in a small bowl. Taste and add more seasoning if needed.

Mix the sour cream sauce ingredients together in a bowl until combined. Taste and add more seasoning if needed.

To serve, layer the potato, eggs and salmon on a plate, then drizzle generously with the sour cream sauce and dill dressing. Garnish with the sliced radishes and dill leaves. Serve cold.

SWEETY

JAMFACE FAVES

Market morsels

MY CHAI

This is a recipe Jono and I came up with when we first opened the cafe, so it's tailored for our palates, but it's up to you how you want to design your brew. I think a lot of you will find the sugar content high but this is how it is traditionally drunk – warm and sweet. In winter you can hit harder with the pepper, for more heat.

3 black peppercorns

4 cloves

8 cardamom pods

2 cinnamon sticks

20 g ginger

4 teaspoons loose-leaf black tea

6 teaspoons raw sugar OR honey, or to taste

250 ml (1 cup) water

250 ml (1 cup) full-cream milk

SERVES 2

GF / V

Using a mortar and pestle, crack the peppercorns, cloves and cardamom pods, but don't grind to a powder. Give the cinnamon and ginger a light bashing, just so everything splits but not too much more.

Combine all the chai ingredients except the milk in a small saucepan. Stir and allow to come to a simmer. Add the milk, stir and bring to a simmer again, then remove from the heat, cover and allow to steep for 7 minutes.

Pour through a fine strainer to remove the tea and spices. Serve hot.

CHILLI-HOISIN CARAMEL APPLE CAKE

This definitely has a push–pull flavour profile, which might polarise some of you. I love watching people tasting this for the first time. Asians tend not to flinch because the boundary between sweet and savoury is more permeable and in fact a defining characteristic of South-East Asian cuisine. You can make this with shiro (white) miso instead of the hoisin sauce, or omit the chilli if that takes you over the edge of yum–yuk.

5 granny smith OR pink lady apples, peeled, cored & finely sliced

300 g unsalted butter, softened

345 g (1½ cups) caster sugar

1 teaspoon vanilla extract OR essence

Pinch of salt

5 large eggs

300 g (2 cups) plain flour, sifted

3 teaspoons baking powder, sifted

35 g (⅓ cup) almond meal, sifted

80 ml (⅓ cup) milk

3 tablespoons sour cream

CARAMEL

3 tablespoons hoisin sauce

4 tablespoons water

310 g (1⅓ cups) caster sugar

1 long red chilli, deseeded & finely sliced, or to taste

MAKES 24 SLICES

V

Preheat the oven to 170°C fan-forced. Line the base and sides of a 30 x 22 cm (or thereabouts) brownie tin with a single sheet of baking paper (otherwise the caramel will leak everywhere). Make sure there's a 2 cm overhang at the top of the tin.

To make the caramel, first mix the hoisin sauce with 1 tablespoon of the water. Mix the sugar and remaining 3 tablespoons of water with a metal spoon in a medium saucepan and bring to the boil. As soon as the caramel turns a pale-golden colour, remove the pan from the heat and immediately whisk in the hoisin sauce mixture and chilli. Be careful, this can get a bit spitty and bubbly. Pour into the prepared tin, then roll the caramel around to coat the base well. Arrange the apple slices in overlapping rows until the base is entirely covered. Allow to cool.

To make the cake batter, in an electric stand mixer fitted with the whisk attachment, cream the butter, sugar, vanilla and salt on the highest speed until pale and fluffy. Add the eggs, one at a time, whisking well between each addition. Fold in the flour, baking powder and almond meal. Whisk the milk and sour cream in a bowl until smooth, then fold into the batter. Spread the mixture evenly over the apple slices and bake for about 40 minutes or until a skewer inserted into the centre of the cake comes out clean.

Allow the cake to cool for 5 minutes, then turn it out onto a serving board. Carefully peel the baking paper off, without disturbing the apple. If any caramel pools down the sides, scoop it up with a rubber spatula and gently spread it back onto the apple. Cool completely before cutting and serving.

The cake stores best unrefrigerated and will keep well for about 3 days if kept in an airtight container.

Work hard and always remember where you came from. I once heard Molly Meldrum say the secret to his success was some sage counsel from his mother to 'never behave as if you are beneath or above anyone'. I love that.

SARAH'S SUPER-PEANUTTY PEANUT COOKIES

These are my most severe and current addiction – super-crisp, super-peanutty biscuits with super-peanutty cream sandwiched between them. Peanut nutters, you'll need to be saved from yourselves.

90 g unsalted butter, softened

90 g (⅓ cup) smooth peanut butter

200 g caster sugar

½ teaspoon bicarbonate of soda

½ teaspoon salt

1 medium egg

280 g plain flour, plus extra for dusting

PEANUT BUTTER CREAM

90 g butter, softened

90 g (⅓ cup) smooth peanut butter

1 tablespoon honey

1 teaspoon vanilla extract OR essence

125 g (1 cup) icing sugar mixture

MAKES ABOUT 25

V

Preheat the oven to 165°C fan-forced. Line a baking tray with baking paper.

Combine the butter, peanut butter, sugar, bicarbonate of soda and salt in the bowl of an electric stand mixer fitted with the whisk attachment, and whisk on the highest speed until pale and fluffy. Add the egg and whisk until smooth. Add the flour and mix with a wooden spoon, then use clean hands to squeeze into a smooth dough.

Shape the dough into discs and roll out on a well-floured work surface until 3 mm thick. Punch out the biscuits using whatever shaped cutter you like, but a peanut-shaped one is adorable! At this point Sarah scores the dough with a chequered pattern for more peanut realism! If you have no cutters, slicing the pastry into rectangles is a perfectly decent solution.

Using an offset spatula, slide the cut shapes onto the prepared tray, leaving 1 cm of space between each one. Bake for 15–20 minutes or until the cookies are very crisp and dry. Cool completely on a wire cooling rack before filling.

To make the peanut butter cream, combine all the ingredients in the bowl of an electric stand mixer fitted with the whisk attachment, and whisk on the highest speed until smooth and fluffy. Transfer the cream to a piping bag and pipe onto the biscuits to sandwich pairs together.

Store the biscuits in an airtight container in the fridge because you don't want the centres to melt in the case of warm weather. They'll keep very well like this for up to a month. Old tins are best for the job!

RASPBERRY JELLY CAKES

I grew up around a lot of baked goods as a kid, but these weren't in Mum's repertoire. I was well into my thirties when I first tasted one, and everything about sinking my teeth into the combination of pink raspberry jelly, the lightest of sponges and snowy-looking coconut instantly evokes childish glee. For Jamface I split the cakes, then sandwich them with raspberry-flavoured cream, but it's not traditional or necessary. You can make all the elements a day ahead but, to exploit the cake at its peak fluffiest, allow it to come to room temp before filling and serving.

1 packet of raspberry jelly crystals

300 ml boiling water

300 ml cool water

7 large eggs

145 g (⅔ cup) caster sugar

1 teaspoon vanilla essence OR raspberry flavouring

Pinch of salt

40 g (⅓ cup) wheaten cornflour

50 g (⅓ cup) self-raising flour

75 g (½ cup) plain flour

270 g (3 cups) desiccated coconut

RASPBERRY CREAM

600 ml thickened cream

60 g (¼ cup) caster sugar

1 teaspoon raspberry flavouring

MAKES 24

Place the jelly crystals and boiling water in a medium bowl and stir to dissolve. Stir in the cool water. Chill in the fridge for about 3 hours until set.

To make the raspberry cream, combine the cream, sugar and raspberry flavouring in the bowl of an electric stand mixer fitted with the whisk attachment, and whisk on the highest speed until stiff peaks form. Cover and chill until needed.

Preheat the oven to 170°C fan-forced. Line the base and sides of a 30 x 22 cm brownie tin with a single sheet of baking paper.

In the bowl of an electric stand mixer fitted with the whisk attachment, combine the eggs, sugar, vanilla or raspberry flavouring and salt, then whisk on the highest speed until the mixture triples in volume. Combine all the flours in a sieve and sift one-third of it over the egg and sugar mixture. Fold very gently until combined. Repeat until all the flours are used, then pour into the prepared tin. Using the back of a spoon, spread the batter so the middle of the rectangle dips in a little, and the edges are mounded a tad higher – this helps the cake to bake with a more even surface. Bake for 15–20 minutes or until a skewer inserted into the centre of the cake comes out clean. Lift the cake out of the tin and cool completely on a wire cooling rack before removing the baking paper. Using a serrated knife, slice the rectangle of sponge into 6 x 4 cm cubes.

Whisk the set jelly well, so it is almost smooth. Cover a baking tray with the coconut, then shake to level. Dip the pieces of sponge into the jelly, making sure all the sides are well covered, then shake the excess off before gently patting on the coconut. Repeat until all the pieces of sponge are coated in jelly and coconut.

Slice the cakes in half and fill with the raspberry cream. Piping is much tidier but using a teaspoon is perfectly fine. Serve at room temperature.

'Tins are still the best way to store baked goods. If you are running low, hit up your local Asian grocer during the Autumn Harvest festival when mooncake tins are aplenty!'

GINGERBREADS & HOW TO ICE THEM WELL

This is a Jamface staple that I get asked about a lot, so here it is for the holiday season or an all-year-round good time! Gingerbread dough can be tricky to handle – it's not just you. You'll find that when it warms up the cracks subside and it gets smoother on rolling, but then harder to handle once you've cut the shapes out. My tip is to use a small offset spatula or butter knife to help transfer the shapes onto the baking trays.

250 g unsalted butter

200 g light brown sugar

2 teaspoons mixed spice

2 tablespoons ground ginger

Good pinch of salt

175 g (½ cup) honey

2 eggs

750 g (5 cups) plain flour, plus extra for dusting

2 teaspoons bicarbonate of soda

ROYAL ICING

125–185 g (1–1½ cups) pure icing sugar, sifted, plus extra for adjusting the texture

1 small egg white

1–2 teaspoons lemon juice

Powder OR gel food colouring of your choice (see Piping Tips & Tricks on page 231)

MAKES ABOUT 50

V

Preheat the oven to 170°C fan-forced. Line two large baking trays with baking paper.

Combine the butter, brown sugar, mixed spice, ground ginger and salt in the bowl of an electric stand mixer fitted with the whisk attachment, and whisk on the highest speed until pale and fluffy. Add the honey and whisk until combined. Add the eggs, one at a time, whisking well between each addition. Sift in the flour and bicarbonate of soda and mix roughly with a wooden spoon, then switch to using clean hands to squeeze the mixture together until well combined. Pat into a disc, cover with cling wrap, then chill for 30 minutes.

Roll the dough out on a well-floured surface, with baking paper on top of the dough, until 4 mm thick. Cut into your chosen shapes and arrange on the baking trays, leaving 5 mm of space between each one. Bake for 10 minutes or until brown. Transfer to wire cooling racks and only decorate them when completely cooled.

To make the royal icing, combine the icing sugar, egg white and lemon juice in a medium bowl and whisk until smooth. Add the colouring and whisk until combined and the texture of toothpaste. Simply whisk in a few more drops of lemon juice if the icing is too stiff, or a tablespoon more icing sugar if it's too runny. This quantity goes a long way – I can pipe about 100 standard biscuits with it. If you want, split the mix into two batches and mix in two different colours. For four colours, double the mixture. Put the icing into plastic piping bags and knot the bags close to the level where the icing reaches. Cut away any excess plastic on top of the knot for easier handling, then cut a 1 mm diameter hole at the other end of the bag. For piping tips and tricks, see page 231.

These store well for up to 3 weeks in an airtight container, but an old biscuit tin is still best!

PIPING TIPS & TRICKS

1. If you are running out of time, forget the colouring and keep the icing classic white – generate interest with shapes instead.

2. If the icing is flowing too fast, it means the hole in the piping bag is too big or the icing is too runny OR both.

3. Cut the tip about 1 mm in diameter for max control and hover the tip just a wee bit above the gingerbread surface for smoother lines. The faster you pipe (it takes a bit of practice) the smoother the lines.

4. Don't waste your icing – it can be refrigerated in the piping bag, stored in an airtight container, to reuse for up to 2 weeks. If the icing looks a bit separated after a long rest in the fridge, massage it in the piping bag until the colour and texture look well combined again.

5. Royal icing needs at least 2 hours to set properly before you pack the gingerbreads into an airtight container or tin.

6. Err on the side of not filling the piping bag past what will fit comfortably in your hand so you have max control – about ½–⅔ cup is best.

7. The most efficient, intense colour comes in the form of food colouring gel or powder and can be found in supermarkets and specialist stores.

SWEETY

COMFORT
COMBOS

Oldies but goodies

PANCAKES WITH BANANA, BUTTERSCOTCH SAUCE & VANILLA SOUR CREAM

You won't believe it but pancakes can be an elusive thing to nail if you aren't aware of a few simple rules. Firstly, don't go nuts mixing the batter or you'll overwork the gluten and also knock out any aeration created by the active ingredients. This equals tough, flat pancakes. Mix only until the batter is just combined and be chill with a few small lumps – in this instance, a smooth batter is your enemy! Also, the idea of banoffee pancakes is so decent, right?

375 ml (1½ cups) milk

3 tablespoons white vinegar

300 g (2 cups) plain flour, sifted

3 teaspoons baking powder, sifted

3 tablespoons caster sugar

½ teaspoon salt

2 teaspoons vanilla extract OR essence

2 eggs

60 g butter, melted, plus a 25 g piece of cold butter with a fork stabbed halfway into it (for greasing the pan)

2 large bananas, peeled & cut into 5 mm thick slices OR use sliced strawberries

BUTTERSCOTCH SAUCE

50 g unsalted butter

100 g brown sugar

3 tablespoons thickened cream

VANILLA SOUR CREAM

250 g (1 cup) sour cream

1 teaspoon vanilla extract OR essence

50 g icing sugar mixture

FEEDS 4

VO

To make the butterscotch sauce, melt the butter and brown sugar in a medium saucepan over medium heat until the sugar is dissolved. Bring to the boil and cook for another minute, then whisk in the cream until well combined. Remove from the heat.

To make the vanilla sour cream, whisk all the ingredients until combined. Chill until needed.

To make the pancake batter, mix the milk and vinegar in a jug. Combine all the dry ingredients in a medium bowl. Add the milk and vinegar mixture to the bowl, along with the vanilla, eggs and melted butter and whisk until just combined – a few tiny lumps is A-okay.

Heat a non-stick frying pan over medium heat and whizz your fork of butter over the surface. Ladle 80 ml (⅓ cup) of the batter into the frying pan and wait for the surface of the pancake to become a little pitted before flipping it over with a spatula. You might have to play around with the heat to get the rate of browning and cooking through right. If you have enough pans, it's a good idea to get two going on the heat so you can use the batter quicker while the active ingredients are most lively. Once the pan is seasoned you can use less butter, which gives the pancakes more caramelisation. Repeat until all the batter is used up.

Serve the pancakes warm with fresh banana or strawberry slices, an indecent amount of the butterscotch sauce and a generous dollop of the vanilla sour cream. There's nothing I hate more than stingy trimmings – you need enough to have with every bite until the end! Don't you agree?

CINNAMON DOUGHNUT DROPS

YES, 'drops' means you can eat more of them. Yes, you could fill these with lemon curd, jam or choc–hazelnut spread but good old-fashioned cinnamon sugar totally floats my boat. Heads up on the batter – it can be made a day ahead and left to rise slowly overnight in the fridge, but be sure there's enough room (three-quarters more space) in the bowl or you'll have a cup overfloweth situ in the morning.

1 teaspoon dry yeast

80 ml (⅓ cup) warm water

70 g butter

440 ml milk

70 g caster sugar

⅛ teaspoon salt

3 eggs

600 g (4 cups) plain flour

2 litres vegetable oil, for deep-frying

CINNAMON SUGAR

230 g (1 cup) caster sugar

2 tablespoons ground cinnamon

MAKES ABOUT 30

V

To make the doughnut batter, mix the yeast and water in a small bowl. Cover with a plate and allow to sit for 10 minutes. Once the mixture has a foamy surface it's ready to use.

Microwave the butter with HALF the milk for 1 minute on high in a heatproof bowl or until the butter is melted. You can also do this in a saucepan on the stove, then remove from the heat. Stir in the sugar until dissolved, then the remaining milk and the salt.

Combine the yeast mixture, butter mixture, eggs and flour in the bowl of an electric stand mixer fitted with the paddle attachment, and beat on the lowest setting for 2 minutes until smooth. Cover the bowl with a damp tea towel and allow the mixture to rest until doubled in volume.

Fill a large piping bag with the batter, securing the end with a rubber band. Snip a 3 cm hole at the tip just before frying.

To make the cinnamon sugar, mix the ingredients together in a bowl.

Pour the vegetable oil into a large saucepan or wok. To test if the oil is ready, rest the tips of a pair of wooden chopsticks on the base of the pan or wok, and if a steady flurry of bubbles rises to the surface, it's ready. If it's very vigorous, it's likely the oil is too hot. Check by squeezing a 3 cm length of batter onto the surface of the oil, then snipping it off with scissors. It should take at least 15 seconds to turn golden brown. Repeat until three-quarters of the surface of the oil is filled with balls of batter – err on the side of overcooking, to make sure the centres are done. Remove from the pan or wok with a spider ladle and drain and cool slightly on a paper towel–lined wire cooling rack. Toss the doughnuts in the cinnamon sugar to coat well and serve immediately.

CREPES, MAPLE SYRUP & VANILLA ICE CREAM (AKA UNI SPECIAL)

This is a something I made a lot in my twenties when Matt and I were povo uni students who couldn't afford anything outside of pantry basics. I was essentially a pretty crap cook, bar desserts. I've recently revived this recipe to rave reviews. It relies on paper-thin crepes that get folded into small parcels filled with vanilla ice cream, which half melts, then marbles with the imperative imitation maple syrup (for old time's sake), and the resulting taste sensation is what the most honest dessert dreams are made of.

CREPES

150 g (1 cup) plain flour

1 tablespoon caster sugar

1 teaspoon vanilla extract OR essence

Pinch of salt

4 large eggs

700 ml milk, plus extra if needed

2 tablespoons vegetable oil

FILLING

500 ml (2 cups) vanilla ice cream

125 ml (½ cup) maple syrup

FEEDS 4

V

To make the crepes, combine the flour, sugar, vanilla, salt, eggs, HALF the milk and the oil in a large bowl and whisk until smooth. Add the remaining milk – and more if you think it needs it. The mixture should look watery and split into droplets when poured from a ladle. If it pours as a smooth band it's probably too thick, BUT you do you, and get it as thin as you can manage.

Heat and lightly grease a 20 cm non-stick frying pan over high heat, so it's almost starting to smoke. Work fast – pour about 80 ml (⅓ cup) of the batter into the pan and roll it around as quickly as you can manage so the surface of the pan is coated. Plug up any holes around the centre. As soon as the edge of the crepe starts to dry up and roll away from the edge of the pan, slide a butter knife between the crepe and pan, then hold the bottom edge with both sets of fingers and swiftly flip the crepe over to cook for a mere second on the other side. The side facing up should be beautifully caramelised (see Tips). Carefully use your fingers to place the crepe on a plate, blonde side up, with no creasing. Repeat until all the batter is used up, piling the crepes on top of one another on a plate.

To stuff the crepes, place a dessertspoon of ice cream and 2 teaspoons of maple syrup in the middle of a crepe. Fold it in half, bring in both sides to the middle, then roll into a parcel. In the spirit of uni-era vibes, these need to be eaten with urgency and the extra parcels are dispensed to the piggy who finishes fastest. If you have extra crepes (unlikely), store them unrefrigerated for up to a day cling-wrapped.

TIPS

It's a bit of a Goldilocks situ with crepes and pan heat. If the crepe batter bubbles up right away, your pan is probably a little too hot.

If the pan is not hot enough or you grease it too heavily, the batter won't bond to the pan surface enough to caramelise – wiping a lightly oiled paper towel on the pan surface is the best method for greasing. You only need to grease the pan every five crepes or thereabouts.

OLD MATE ORANGE & APPLE TEA CAKE

A good tea cake is like an old friend – familiar, comforting and rarely lets you down. And it's my old friend, Sarah, who's given me this recipe. Incidentally, she has also illustrated it! Sitting in the morning sun with a slice of this for brekky with a cup of hot black tea and magpies warbling nearby is my idea of paradise. This is a 'bung in and mix' affair so I'm calling to attention all the hopeless bakers out there – this one's got yer name on it! As for the combo of apples, orange and sultanas, it's a solid!

200 g (1⅓ cups) plain flour, sifted

2 teaspoons baking powder, sifted

½ teaspoon bicarbonate of soda, sifted

150 g (¾ cup) caster sugar

Generous pinch of salt

1 large pink lady or granny smith apple, peeled, cored & roughly chopped

2 large eggs

1 teaspoon vanilla extract OR essence

125 ml (½ cup) vegetable OR olive oil

125 g (½ cup) Greek yoghurt

Finely grated zest of 1 orange

80 g (½ cup) sultanas OR 5 mm diced dried apricots

Icing sugar mixture, for dusting

FEEDS 10–12

V

Preheat the oven to 170°C fan-forced. Grease and flour a 22 cm ring cake tin.

Combine the dry ingredients except the sultanas or dried apricots and icing sugar mixture in a medium bowl and whisk briefly to combine. Add all the wet ingredients and stir gently with a whisk until just combined. Fold in the sultanas or apricots and pour into the prepared tin.

Bake for about 40 minutes or until a skewer inserted into the centre of the cake comes out clean. Immediately demould, while still hot, onto a plate, then quickly flip it so it's sitting right side up again, onto a wire cooling rack. Cool completely and dust with icing sugar mixture before serving.

CLASSIC VANILLA CUSTARD TART

There is no one who doesn't love this classic. Does it even need an introduction? I think not. I might just forewarn the novice or impatient baker that speeding up the cook time is no good. The slow and low method guarantees the most satin-smooth finish on the baked custard, which is important because a finer texture enables literal inhalation of the final product.

3 eggs, plus 1 extra for sealing the pastry case

2 teaspoons vanilla extract OR essence

3 tablespoons caster sugar

500 ml (2 cups) thickened cream

3 tablespoons milk

Freshly grated nutmeg

ORANGE & ALMOND PASTRY

180 g caster sugar

100 g (1 cup) almond meal

260 g (1¾ cups) plain flour, plus extra for dusting

⅛ teaspoon salt

Finely grated zest of ½ orange

200 g chilled unsalted butter, diced into 2 cm pieces

1 small egg

FEEDS UP TO 14

VO

Combine the eggs, vanilla and sugar in a medium mixing bowl and whisk until just combined. Gently whisk in the cream and milk (because mad whisking equals bubbles and a bumpy finish) then allow the mixture to rest at room temperature until needed.

To make the pastry, place the sugar, almond meal, flour, salt, orange zest and butter in a food processor and pulse until sandy. Add the egg and pulse until the mixture comes together. Tip the dough onto a clean work surface and squeeze into a 2 cm thick disc (the thicker this is, the more rolling later). Wrap in cling wrap and chill for 30 minutes.

Preheat the oven to 170°C fan-forced. Line just the base of a round 26 cm tart tin, with a removable base, with baking paper.

Roll the pastry out on a floured surface into a 4 mm thick circle and carefully line the prepared tart tin. If it breaks or cracks, don't worry – simply patch and press together and it will seal on baking. Using the edge of the tin as a guide, pinch away any excess pastry. Stab all over the base with a fork at 4 cm intervals, then pop it in the freezer for 20 minutes.

Blind bake* the tart shell for about 20 minutes or until evenly golden. If the base has bubbled up, immediately use a clean oven mitt to press down gently and release the trapped air while the pastry is hot. Whisk the extra egg and baste the base and edge of the tart shell generously – do two coats. Cool before filling with the custard mixture. Reduce the oven temperature to 120°C.

If the surface of the custard is bubbly, wave a blowtorch over it and the bubbles will burst. If you don't have a blowtorch, don't worry too much – it's just a cosmetic issue. Bake for 1 hour or until the custard is just set and still a little wobbly but not rippling under the surface. Cool completely before slicing. This is best eaten on the day but is still decent when refrigerated for up to 2 days if covered well.

*Blind baking is simply baking a pastry shell on its own before either filling it with fresh ingredients or, in this case, with raw ingredients that need further cooking.

SWEETY

ASIAN
FLAVES

Coconut caper

COCONUT RICE PUDDING WITH JACKFRUIT & LYCHEES

If you love the traditional flavours of South-East Asian desserts, this is a really simple way to get a fix. Please note medium-grain rice is a must. Any long-grain varieties will break and won't deliver that creaminess you want with a rice pudding. You can use short-grain varieties like arborio and koshihikari, but add another 125 ml (½ cup) of liquid and another 10–15 minutes to the cooking time. Swap out the coconut cream for more milk if you like, and play away with flavours – there are endless permutations. One of my faves gives the pud a Middle Eastern spin. Just sub out the Asian flavours with rosewater, then add strawberries and a sprinkle of roasted pistachios to finish.

750 ml (3 cups) milk

250 ml (1 cup) coconut cream

80 g (⅓ cup) caster sugar

¼ teaspoon pandan aroma pasta (found at Asian grocers)

Pinch of salt

160 g (¾ cup) medium-grain rice

½ tin lychees, halved*

½ tin jackfruit, sliced into 5 mm pieces

4 scoops of vanilla ice cream (optional)

FEEDS 4

GF / V

Preheat the oven to 170°C fan-forced.

Combine the milk, coconut cream and caster sugar in a saucepan over medium heat. Heat and stir only until the sugar is dissolved – don't boil. Stir in the pandan, salt and rice.

Transfer the mixture to a 2 litre baking dish with a lid (or cover snugly with foil) and bake for about 30–40 minutes, stirring well halfway through the cooking time. Taste the rice to make sure it is tender – don't worry if there seems to be a fair amount of liquid left as the rice will quickly absorb it while resting.

Divide the rice pudding among four bowls and top each with two or three lychees and some jackfruit pieces. Serve hot or at room temperature with a scoop of vanilla ice cream, if desired. Leftovers can be kept in the fridge for up to 3 days and warmed up in the microwave.

*To make the lychee flowers, use a small pair of scissors to snip from the opening to three-quarters of the way towards the bottom of the lychee, into six segments. Unfurl gently to splay the petals out.

TEENA'S VIETNAMESE SWEET MUNG BEAN & COCONUT SOUP (LEK TAU SUAN)

I'm not quite sure how to describe this without it sounding completely gross. It's what a lot of Asian cultures have for dessert and the Chinese call *tong soii*, which translates to 'sugar water', and essentially is a dessert soup (ermergahd, this explanation is so not working). Could you just trust me when I say it's one of my fave sweet things made by my sister-in-law Teena and is absolutely delicious? Also, mung beans are preferable but, honestly, unless you're a pulse connoisseur, dried red beans, dried yellow or green lentils, or even dried yellow or green peas, will all work.

230 g mung beans, soaked in cold water overnight

1.5 litres water

50 g water chestnut powder (found at Asian grocers)

2 tablespoons water

100 g water chestnuts, roughly chopped

¼ teaspoon salt

400 ml tin coconut milk

PANDAN SYRUP

1.5 litres water

200 g sugar

6 pandan leaves (found in the freezer section of Asian grocers), torn lengthways into thin strips, then knotted together

FEEDS 4–6

GF / DF / VG

Rinse the mung beans then drain them well in a sieve for about 10 minutes.

Meanwhile, bring the water to the boil, then add the mung beans and boil until just tender and NO MORE or you'll have mush. Rinse in cool water, then drain well in a sieve until needed.

To make the pandan syrup, place all the ingredients in a large saucepan and bring to the boil, stirring until the sugar dissolves. Remove from the heat.

In a small bowl mix the water chestnut powder and water into a smooth paste. Ladle in about 250 ml (1 cup) of the hot pandan syrup and whisk until well combined. Add this to the rest of the syrup and whisk until smooth. Stir in the mung beans, water chestnuts and salt.

Serve hot with a few tablespoons of the coconut milk drizzled onto every serve.

VAL'S VIETNAMESE HONEYCOMB CAKE (BÁNH BÒ NUÓNG)

I just dig bouncy mouthfeel things and desserts are no exception. If you love pandan flavour, like most do, you'll enjoy this moreish tea cake that gets its name from the curious tunnels that line the cross-section of the cake. For the non-bakers, I have great news – this cake requires minimal technique yet near to guaranteed success!

250 ml (1 cup) coconut milk

150 g (⅔ cup) caster sugar

½ teaspoon pandan aroma pasta (found at Asian grocers)

½ teaspoon salt

1 tablespoon vegetable oil

5 large eggs

160 g tapioca flour*

10 g rice flour

2 teaspoons cream of tartar

1 teaspoon bicarbonate of soda

FEEDS 10

GF / DF / V

Grease a round 20 cm (NOT non-stick) cake tin with vegetable oil. Place in the oven to preheat at 180°C fan-forced.

Combine the coconut milk, sugar, pandan and salt in a small heatproof bowl and microwave on high for 1 minute. Add the vegetable oil and stir until the sugar is dissolved.

Crack the eggs into a large bowl. Press the tip of a whisk into the yolks to burst them, then sift in the tapioca and rice flours, cream of tartar and bicarbonate of soda. Whisk until just smooth, then add the coconut milk mixture and whisk again to combine. Pass the batter through a sieve to press out any lumps, making sure to scrape the bottom of the sieve to include all the mixture. Whisk once again then pour into the heated cake tin. Drop the cake tin onto a work surface from a 5 cm height, several times, to be rid of bubbles.

Bake for 35 minutes or until the surface of the cake springs back easily when gently pressed. Immediately invert the cake tin onto a wire cooling rack. When completely cooled, run a paring knife around the edge of the tin to release the cake, then, using your fingers, gently and gradually tease the bottom of the cake away from the tin. This will feel wrong but persist – the texture of this particular cake tolerates the manhandling! Sometimes the cake will unmould itself. In this instance, immediately flip it so it's right side up again – otherwise you'll squish all those beautiful tunnels.

This cake stores beautifully at room temperature in an airtight container for up to 2 days, but I doubt it'll last that long!

*I find Asian brands work best.

Using the microwave has a
mysterious advantage.

Making custards?

Make custards to the usual recipe
but where you would normally
cook over a stove, instead cook in
a heatproof bowl in the microwave
in 2-minute bursts.

Split a custard or curd?

Don't panic! Blitz it in a blender or with a stick blender and nine times out of ten
it should re-emulsify (become smooth again). If it doesn't work, you've positively murdered it
and it might be back to square one unless you don't mind a slightly 'textured' result.

HAWAIIAN BUTTER MOCHI CAKE

Easy-peasy, chewy, bouncy, delicious joy. Mochi, but buttery and baked,
with a gorgeous salty coconut crust.

170 g unsalted butter, melted

400 ml tin coconut milk

300 g glutinous rice flour (found in
the Asian section of supermarkets or
at Asian grocers)

150 g tapioca flour*

1½ teaspoons baking powder

460 g (2 cups) caster sugar

1 teaspoon salt

500 ml (2 cups) milk

4 large eggs

2 teaspoons vanilla extract OR essence

30 g (½ cup) shredded coconut

A few pinches of salt flakes

MAKES 24 PIECES

GF / V

Preheat the oven to 170°C fan-forced. Grease a brownie tin or baking dish
that is roughly 26 x 20 cm.

Combine the melted butter, coconut milk, glutinous rice flour, tapioca flour,
baking powder, sugar and salt in a large bowl. Whisk until smooth. Add the
milk, eggs and vanilla and whisk until well combined. Drop the mixing bowl
from a 10 cm height onto a work surface to be rid of any bubbles, then pour
the mixture into the prepared tin or dish. Sprinkle the coconut and salt
flakes evenly over the surface.

Bake for about 1 hour until the top is golden brown and the centre of the
cake springs back easily when pressed gently. Cool completely in the tin
or dish before cutting into squares. Store for up to 3 days in an airtight
container at room temperature and in the fridge for about a week.
Microwave on high for about 10 seconds per piece to soften.

*I find Asian brands work best.

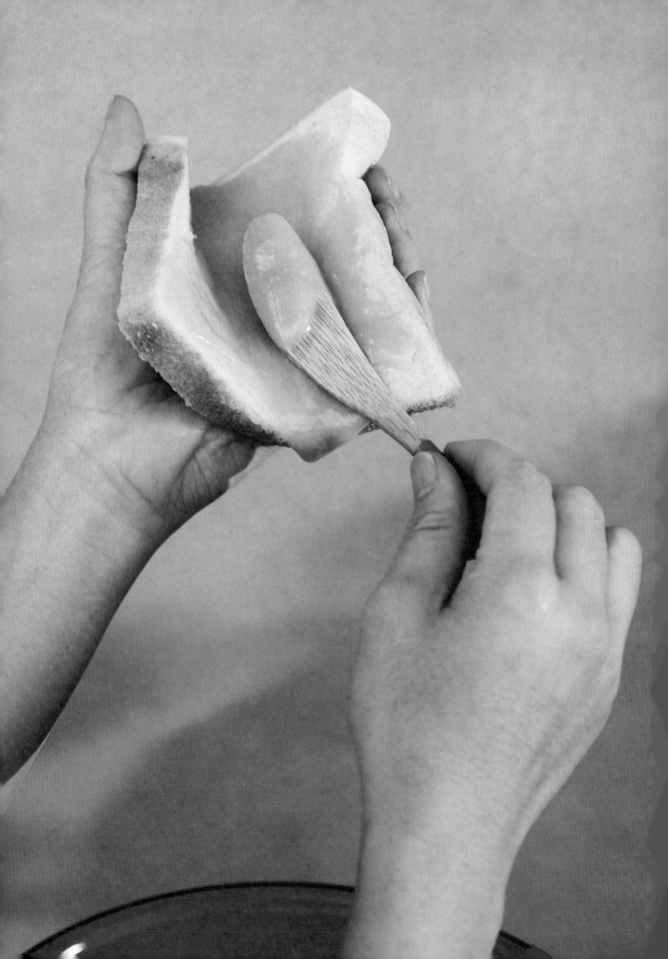

6-MINUTE MICROWAVE KAYA – MALAYSIAN COCONUT JAM (YAAAARSE! 'TIS TRUE!)

If you make this the traditional way like my mum does, it literally takes 2 hours. And to that I say WHY? when it only takes 6 minutes in the microwave. It's hands-down my fave thing to slather on fresh sliced white bread (the most heinously processed kind) – in such excessive amounts that some always ends up plopping on the kitchen floor after I take the first bite. In Malaysia, kaya is most famously served as brekky on thick-cut toast with butter. And if you want to turn it into a dessert snack, you can steam a slab of sticky rice with salty coconut milk, slice it into bite-sized diamonds and pipe a dollop of kaya on top – an absolute winner!

5 extra-large eggs

500 g caster sugar

300 ml coconut cream

6 pandan leaves (found in the freezer section of Asian grocers), torn lengthways into strips, then knotted into 2 small bunches

MAKES ABOUT 1 LITRE

GF / DF / V

In a large microwave-safe bowl, whisk the eggs, sugar and coconut cream until well combined. Submerge the pandan leaves in the mixture, then microwave on high for 3 minutes, then again for another 3 minutes or until thickened, whisking well between bursts. This goes against everything you are usually taught about curd, but when using this method, you actually WANT the kaya to look curdled. If it doesn't, I'd go another 2 minutes, then blitz the crap out of it with a stick blender until smooth. This ensures it's cooked properly and will set nicely in the fridge.

Allow to cool completely, with the pandan still submerged, then remove the pandan before storing the kaya in clean, sterilised jars*. The kaya will keep for up to 3 weeks refrigerated.

*To sterilise jars, boil the jars and lids (not screwed on), completely submerged in water, for 10 minutes. Dry them upside down on a clean wire cooling rack completely before using.

To keep the edge of a cake, where icing meets plate, clean ...

Tuck thin strips of baking paper under the edge of the cake, ice then carefully pull them away and discard.

PANDAN SWISS ROLL WITH COCONUT JAM

Not the most attractive cake around, but for me, the smell of a freshly baked pandan sponge with kaya is the most comforting cocoon of fond memories – spending time next to Mum in the kitchen on weekends, when I got schooled hard on how to measure ingredients with sniper-like precision, deftly fold flour into a sponge mixture, and line a cake tin like nobody's business.

4 large eggs

80 g (⅓ cup) caster sugar

½ teaspoon pandan aroma pasta (found at Asian grocers)

Pinch of salt

1 teaspoon baking powder, sifted

100 g (⅔ cup) plain flour, sifted

1 x quantity 6-Minute Microwave Kaya (page 257)

FEEDS ABOUT 10

DF / V

Preheat the oven to 170°C fan-forced. Line the base and sides of a 30 x 23 x 2 cm baking tray with baking paper.

Place the eggs, sugar, pandan and salt in the bowl of an electric stand mixer fitted with the whisk attachment, and whisk on the highest speed until the mixture triples in volume. Add the baking powder and HALF the flour, then fold very gently until combined. Repeat with the remaining flour.

Spread the mixture evenly in the prepared baking tray and bake for about 15 minutes or until golden and the centre springs back when gently pressed.

Working quickly, tip the cake, top-side down, onto a clean tea towel and remove the baking paper. Use the tea towel to help shield your hands from the heat and roll it up snugly, along the longest side, into a sausage while still hot or it will split. Cool before gently unravelling just enough to generously slather the inside surface with kaya.

Serve at room temperature and best eaten on the day.

SWEETY

SHOW STOPPERS

Ooh! Aah!

FLOATING ISLANDS (ÎLE FLOTTANTE)

This is an oldie but goodie that I love resurrecting for dinner parties. The meringue recipe is from my late friend Emmanuel Mollois, who I miss incredibly. I was shocked he microwaved instead of poached the meringue in milk, seeing as he was, OF COURSE, a stickler for tradition, but it's so much more foolproof. What you get is ethereally textured meringue sitting in chilled orange custard, with pleasantly bitter shards of caramel and burnished flakes of almond – elegance personified. Like eating a cloud.

4 egg whites

Pinch of salt

80 g (⅓ cup) caster sugar

3 tablespoons toasted flaked OR slivered almonds*

CUSTARD

250 ml (1 cup) milk**

250 ml (1 cup) thickened cream**

Finely grated zest of ½ orange

4 egg yolks

70 g caster sugar

CARAMEL

80 g (⅓ cup) caster sugar

FEEDS 4

GF / VO

**For a more luxurious result you can use a total of 500 ml (2 cups) of cream, rather than half cream and half milk.

Place the egg whites and salt in the bowl of a stand mixer fitted with the whisk attachment. Whisk on the highest speed until medium peaks form, then add the sugar, a tablespoon at a time, whisking well between additions, until you have stiff peaks and no residual grains of sugar can be felt when you rub the mixture between your fingers.

Shape about 80 ml (⅓ cup) of the meringue into a rough sphere or football shape using two large metal spoons and place on a heatproof plate. Fit as many of these on the plate as possible, leaving a 2 cm gap between them. Lightly drape a piece of cling wrap over the top and microwave on high for about 30 seconds or until the meringue doesn't collapse when gently pressed. You can leave the meringues to cool, then store them in a container in the fridge if you're making this a few hours ahead. Otherwise set aside at room temperature until needed.

To make the custard, combine the milk, cream and orange zest in a heatproof bowl and microwave on high for 2–3 minutes. In another bowl, whisk the egg yolks and sugar until pale and fluffy. Add to the heated milk and cream and whisk well. Microwave for 2 minutes on high, then again in 1-minute bursts, whisking very well in between, until the mixture thickens enough to coat the back of a wooden spoon without running off immediately. If you split (curdle) the custard, pour it into a blender and blend on the highest speed and it should re-emulsify. If not, you've lived too dangerously and should probably start again from scratch. Cover the custard and chill until needed.

To make the caramel, mix the sugar with a dash of water in a small saucepan over medium heat. Boil until the mixture starts to turn golden, then watch it like a hawk. You want the colour of strong tea, but it happens in the blink of an eye, so whisk it off the stove just before it reaches that colour. Move with urgency here. With a rubber spatula, scoop small amounts (about 2 teaspoons) of the mixture and smear it as thinly as possible onto baking paper. You can make these a day ahead and snip around each shape. Store them piled on top of one another, unrefrigerated, in an airtight container, then peel off the paper as you plate.

FLOATING ISLANDS (ÎLE FLOTTANTE)
(CONT.)

To serve, ladle about 125 ml (½ cup) of the custard into bowls, then float two of the poached meringues on top. Finish with a sprinkle of the toasted almonds and balance a thin shard of caramel on the meringues.

*Nuts can be toasted in a few different ways:

1. On a baking tray in a single layer in a 165–170°C fan-forced oven until the edges are golden brown (about 15 minutes).

2. In a dry frying pan in a single layer over medium heat until the edges are golden brown.

3. Microwaved in 1-minute bursts on high in a heatproof bowl stirring after every burst, until the edges are golden brown. If toasting whole nuts, use your sense of smell. When they smell appropriately 'roasty', cut one open to check – microwaved nuts roast from the centre outwards.

4. Also, if you want a quick savoury snack, atomise any raw nuts with a little water, then toss in your seasoning of choice and microwave until 'roasted'. Use your intuition as all nuts roast at different rates based on their size and oil content.

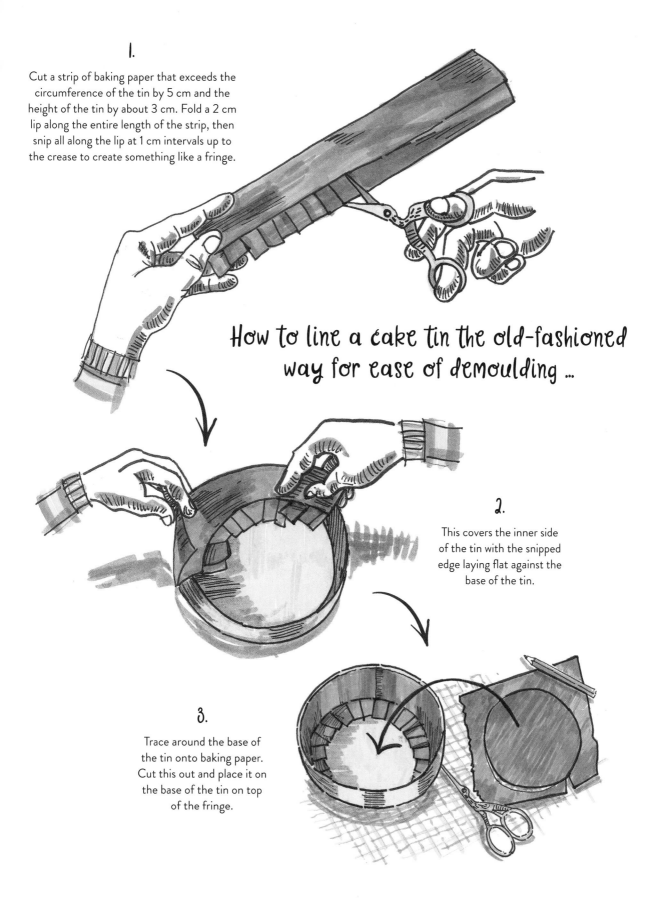

1.

Cut a strip of baking paper that exceeds the circumference of the tin by 5 cm and the height of the tin by about 3 cm. Fold a 2 cm lip along the entire length of the strip, then snip all along the lip at 1 cm intervals up to the crease to create something like a fringe.

How to line a cake tin the old-fashioned way for ease of demoulding ...

2.

This covers the inner side of the tin with the snipped edge laying flat against the base of the tin.

3.

Trace around the base of the tin onto baking paper. Cut this out and place it on the base of the tin on top of the fringe.

SARAH'S STRAWBERRIES & CREAM TART

When it comes to desserts, it's vibrant seasonal fruit paired with pastry and cream or custard that gets me every time. This is a Jamface favourite that Sarah makes, and it's the simple layering of strawberry flavour in the compote and cream, then fresh fruit, that makes it the most straightforward kind of delectable. This pastry is one I swear by because it rarely shrinks and it's incredibly forgiving. If you split it when lining the tin, simply patch with a small amount of pastry and press to seal the cracked parts together – they will bake out nicely.

1 x quantity Orange & Almond Pastry (page 242)

STRAWBERRY COMPOTE

100 g strawberries (fresh or frozen), hulled & cut into 5 mm thick slices

100 g caster sugar

STRAWBERRY CREAM

400 ml thickened cream

50 g caster sugar

1–2 teaspoons strawberry essence

TO SERVE

2 x 250 g punnets of strawberries

Edible flowers, for decorating

Mint leaves, for decorating (optional)

FEEDS ABOUT 12

VO

To make the strawberry compote, combine the strawberries and sugar in a medium saucepan and bring to the boil. Reduce to a simmer and cook, stirring continuously, for about 1 minute. Blend to a puree, then chill before using.

Preheat the oven to 170°C fan-forced. Line just the base of a round 26 cm tart tin with baking paper.

Roll the pastry out on a lightly floured work surface until 4 mm thick. Line the tart tin with the pastry, making sure to press the pastry in well. Using the edge of the tin as a guide, pinch the excess pastry away and freeze the leftover bits*. Stab all over the base with a fork at 4 cm intervals, then freeze the pastry for 20 minutes.

Blind bake** the tart shell for about 20 minutes or until deep golden. If the base has bubbled up, immediately use a clean oven mitt to press down gently and release the trapped air while the pastry is hot. Leave the tart shell in the tin to cool completely before transferring to a serving plate to fill.

To make the strawberry cream, whisk the cream, sugar and strawberry essence until stiff.

To assemble the tart, spread enough strawberry cream to fill the tart shell to three-quarters of the height. Arrange the strawberry slices in concentric circles until the cream is covered. To finish, spoon or pipe the strawberry compote evenly over the top, then decorate with edible flowers and mint leaves, if desired. Serve the tart with the remaining cream and compote.

*This can be rolled out, cut and baked into biscuits. The pastry can be premade and stored as a disc in the freezer for up to 2 months if cling-wrapped and then placed in a sealed ziplock bag.

**Blind baking is simply baking a pastry shell on its own before either filling it with fresh ingredients or with raw ingredients that then need further cooking.

LYCHEE CHIFFON CAKE WITH WHITE CHOCOLATE MATCHA GANACHE

It seems impossible for me to write a cookbook without including a chiffon cake, because texturally it's just the most sumptuous cake in the world, and in my opinion it dacks on even the most expertly made sponge. Here's yet another delicious incarnation of it – lychee, matcha and white chocolate – also a Jamface favourite. But may I add that it's a real bummer to transport on account of its mind-blowingly impressive height. Heads up on the ganache – it's best to make it the night before so it's properly chilled, or you'll have issues whipping it to stiff peaks.

5 large eggs, separated, plus 3 extra egg whites

150 g (⅔ cup) caster sugar

210 ml coconut cream

80 ml (⅓ cup) vegetable oil

1 tablespoon Paraiso lychee liqueur

150 g (1 cup) plain flour

2 teaspoons baking powder

Pinch of salt

½ teaspoon cream of tartar

1 tin lychees, drained & diced into 5 mm pieces

MATCHA GANACHE

200 g white chocolate, chopped

250 ml (1 cup) thickened cream

Pinch of salt

A few drops of green food colouring (optional)

3 teaspoons matcha powder, sifted

LYCHEE CREAM

600 ml thickened cream

70 g caster sugar

1 tablespoon Paraiso lychee liqueur

FEEDS ABOUT 14

VO

To make the ganache, combine the white chocolate, cream and salt in a heatproof bowl and microwave for 1–2 minutes on high. Whisk until smooth, then cover with cling wrap and refrigerate overnight or for a minimum of 4 hours.

Preheat the oven to 170°C fan-forced.

Combine the egg yolks, HALF the sugar, the coconut cream, vegetable oil, liqueur, flour, baking powder and salt in a large bowl and whisk until smooth.

Place all the egg whites and cream of tartar in the bowl of an electric stand mixer fitted with the whisk attachment, and whisk on the highest speed until medium peaks form. Add the remaining sugar in two batches, whisking well between additions, until stiff peaks form.

Add one-third of the meringue to the yolk mixture and stir gently with a whisk until combined. Add the remaining meringue and stir gently until incorporated.

Pour the mixture into a 25 cm aluminium angel food cake tin with a removable base (it's important that it's NOT non-stick and definitely no greasing please). Bake for about 45 minutes or until a skewer inserted into the centre of the cake comes out clean. Remove the cake from the oven and immediately invert the tin on its little legs. Cool completely before carefully running a knife around the inner and outer edges to remove the bottom of the tin, then slicing as close to the base as possible to release the cake.

Place the chilled ganache and colouring (if using) in the bowl of an electric stand mixer fitted with the whisk attachment, and whisk on the highest speed until the texture of whipped butter. Mix in the matcha powder with a spatula* until combined. Cover and chill until needed.

*You need to use a spatula as vigorous whisking will cause the matcha to split the ganache.

LYCHEE CHIFFON CAKE WITH
WHITE CHOCOLATE MATCHA GANACHE (CONT.)

To make the lychee cream, combine the cream, sugar and lychee liqueur in the bowl of an electric stand mixer fitted with the whisk attachment, and whisk on the highest speed until stiff peaks form. Cover and chill until needed.

To assemble the cake, first cut a vertical notch from the bottom to the top of the cake (see Tip opposite) to keep the layers in the same position as you originally sliced them. Slice the cake into three even layers, horizontally. Place the bottom layer on a serving plate and spread about 180 ml (¾ cup) of the lychee cream evenly over the surface to cover. Scatter HALF the diced lychees evenly over the cream. Place the next cake layer on top, lining up the vertical notches, and repeat with the cream and lychees as on the first layer. Place the final cake layer on top, making sure the vertical notches line up once more. Cover the entire cake evenly with the matcha ganache, then decorate the cake however you wish with the remaining lychee cream. It's best served immediately at room temperature but can be kept chilled overnight.

'Having trouble cutting a cake into even layers for filling?
Cut a vertical notch on the side and match the layers back
after filling, so they return to their original position and the
cake stays level.'

STRAWBERRIES, MASCARPONE YOGHURT CREAM & BALSAMIC CARAMEL

This genius Italian combo of something creamy and vanilla flavoured with strawberries and balsamic is nothing short of a culinary phenomenon. You'd think the sourness of the strawberries with the sharpness of the yoghurt and balsamic would get a bit much, but some kind of sorcery happens when it all comes together on the palate ... the bonus being that it takes no time to put together. And do take the basil leaves seriously because they add such a beguiling savoury note to the dish.

2 x 250 g punnets of strawberries, hulled & halved OR 4 blood oranges, peeled & segmented

80 g (½ cup) roasted almonds, roughly chopped

Handful of baby basil leaves, to serve

MASCARPONE YOGHURT CREAM

240 g (1 cup) mascarpone

260 g (1 cup) Greek yoghurt

1–2 teaspoons vanilla extract OR essence

100–120 g icing sugar mixture

BALSAMIC CARAMEL

80 g unsalted butter

100 g brown sugar

3 tablespoons balsamic vinegar

FEEDS 4

GF / V

To make the mascarpone yoghurt cream, whisk all the ingredients together in a bowl and chill until needed.

To make the balsamic caramel, melt the butter and brown sugar in a small saucepan over medium–low heat until the sugar is dissolved. Stir in the balsamic vinegar and simmer for 30 seconds, then cool completely before using.

To serve, divide the mascarpone yoghurt cream among four bowls, load the strawberries on top, then drizzle with a generous amount of the balsamic caramel. Finish with a sprinkling of roasted almonds and baby basil leaves.

Flathead with burnt butter, lemon & caper sauce, recipe on page 118

CONVERSION CHARTS

Measuring cups and spoons may vary slightly from one country to another, but the difference is generally not enough to affect a recipe. All cup and spoon measures are level.

One Australian metric measuring cup holds 250 ml (8 fl oz), one Australian tablespoon holds 20 ml (4 teaspoons) and one Australian metric teaspoon holds 5 ml. North America, New Zealand and the UK use a 15 ml (3-teaspoon) tablespoon.

LENGTH

METRIC	IMPERIAL
3 mm	⅛ inch
6 mm	¼ inch
1 cm	½ inch
2.5 cm	1 inch
5 cm	2 inches
18 cm	7 inches
20 cm	8 inches
23 cm	9 inches
25 cm	10 inches
30 cm	12 inches

LIQUID MEASURES

ONE AMERICAN PINT	ONE IMPERIAL PINT
500 ml (16 fl oz)	600 ml (20 fl oz)

CUP	METRIC	IMPERIAL
⅛ cup	30 ml	1 fl oz
¼ cup	60 ml	2 fl oz
⅓ cup	80 ml	2½ fl oz
½ cup	125 ml	4 fl oz
⅔ cup	160 ml	5 fl oz
¾ cup	180 ml	6 fl oz
1 cup	250 ml	8 fl oz
2 cups	500 ml	16 fl oz
2¼ cups	560 ml	20 fl oz
4 cups	1 litre	32 fl oz

DRY MEASURES

The most accurate way to measure dry ingredients is to weigh them. However, if using a cup, add the ingredient loosely to the cup and level with a knife; don't compact the ingredient unless the recipe requests 'firmly packed'.

METRIC	IMPERIAL
15 g	½ oz
30 g	1 oz
60 g	2 oz
125 g	4 oz (¼ lb)
185 g	6 oz
250 g	8 oz (½ lb)
375 g	12 oz (¾ lb)
500 g	16 oz (1 lb)
1 kg	32 oz (2 lb)

OVEN TEMPERATURES

CELSIUS	FAHRENHEIT
100°C	200°F
120°C	250°F
150°C	300°F
160°C	325°F
180°C	350°F
200°C	400°F
220°C	425°F

CELSIUS	GAS MARK
110°C	¼
130°C	½
140°C	1
150°C	2
170°C	3
180°C	4
190°C	5
200°C	6
220°C	7
230°C	8
240°C	9
250°C	10

Big fat thank yous to ...

The long-suffering Mary Small – I bet you regret sticking your neck out for ol' mayhem Magoo over here! I know it has been harrowing not AT times but MOST of the time, yet you have been the most amazing hype girl from beginning to end. I don't think I'll ever find a publisher who gets me as much as you do. I treasure that beautiful maze of a mind map you presented to me in the early days – it stands as a rare moment in my life where I felt completely understood in all my madness.

Jane Winning, thank you for reigning in the chaos with such endurance. Despite having one of the most calming voices I've ever encountered, at times I was certain I could hear your hands miming a violent strangulation at the other end the phone and I don't blame you at all. So many well-intended conversations about deadlines and then I would proceed to meet none. You have been a model of patience and empathy.

Kirby Armstrong, for so beautifully knitting together this graphic circus of a book!

Ariana Klepac, for smoothing out the boo boos, dealing with my stubborn ideas and creating order in my words.

Sarah Rich, for your hilarious and sensitive illustrations and also your quiet but stoic friendship.

Henry Trumble, thank you for your mad skilz but almost equally important on those days that stretched an eternity, your cheerful countenance and unrelenting patience. It was 'gorge' to collaborate and bring so much 'tent-sian' to ALL the pages! Also, you should probably include 'bottomless pit' on your business card because it's a proper asset on food shoots.

Jack Fenby, thank you for your utmost professionalism and not complaining once even tho 10 minutes usually meant 25, and for being 'Insinkerator II' – we know how much I hate food waste.

Gretl Watson-Blazewicz, thank you for those gorgeous captures of me and the mutts – working with you is always effortless.

Mandy Hall, I'm certain I made you feel like Medusa most days of the shoot, yet your kindness and humour prevailed! I know I nearly killed you with those crazy hours, but I'm glad we agree the result is perfectly joyous if a little nuts. I'm so grateful for our sisterhood, otherwise prawngate could have ended in fisticuffs – not a good look on day 2. Never stop loving so purely and deeply.

Matthew Phipps, my partner in crime, it's your turn next.

INDEX

6-minute microwave kaya – Malaysian coconut jam 257

A

Afghan-style rice with cauliflower or chicken 202
almonds
    Cassie Lee's no-cook tomato sauce 24
    Chilli–hoisin caramel apple cake 218
    Floating islands (île flottante) 265–6
    green beans & almonds 118
    orange & almond pastry 242, 268
    pesto 53
    Strawberries, mascarpone yoghurt cream & balsamic caramel 274
anchovies
    anchovy & garlic paste 167
    bagna cauda 171
    Cavatelli with anchovy butter & fresh tomato 167
    T-bone steak with bagna cauda & charred fennel 171
    Tomato, burrata, anchovies & balsamic 48
    Zen's creamy zucchini & ancho pasta sauce 174
apples
    Chilli–hoisin caramel apple cake 218
    green apple & chilli relish 160
Asian slaw 193–4
asparagus
    Asparagus, hollandaise, eggs & ham 180–1
    Prawn & asparagus risotto with burnt sage butter 177
Avgolemono 60
avocados
    Grilled chicken tortillas with charred corn, kiwi salsa & jalapeno cream 208
    Hand-rolled sushi 138
    Life-changing guacamole 34

B

Babaganoush 205
bagna cauda 171
balsamic caramel 274
banana leaf baskets 193–4
bananas: Pancakes with banana, butter scotch sauce & vanilla sour cream 235
Bánh bò nướng (Val's Vietnamese honey comb cake) 250

beans
    Chicken, long bean & preserved olive stir-fry 90
    green beans & almonds 118
    Teena's Vietnamese sweet mung bean & coconut soup (lek tau suan) 248
beef
    Fast pho 70
    T-bone steak with bagna cauda & charred fennel 171
beetroot: Comforting kale, coconut & beetroot curry 76
beurre manié 178
blind baking 242, 268
bok choy
    Meltdown ramen 28
    Prawn & pork balls, glass vermicelli in fragrant coconut sauce 156
    Sesame omelette soup with rice vermicelli 63
Brazilian cheese bread (pão de queijo) 40
bread
    Brazilian cheese bread (pão de queijo) 40
    Israeli pita 204
    Sourdough bread 14–5
broccoli: Not-boring roasted broccoli & sweet potato 22
broccolini
    Miso-glazed salmon or eggplant with crunchy greens 100
    Steamed ginger chicken with lapcheong & shiitake mushrooms 82
buns, Mama Yeow's sweet pork 124
burnt sage butter 122
butterscotch sauce 235

C

cabbage
    Asian slaw 193–4
    Kimchi, fried seaweed, rice 42
    Margaret's curry cashew slaw 146.
    Meltdown ramen 28
    Pork & kimchi dumplings with Thai chilli jam 126
cakes
    Chilli–hoisin caramel apple cake 218
    cutting tips 272–3
    Hawaiian butter mochi cake 254
    icing tips 258
    lining cake tins 267
    Lychee chiffon cake with white chocolate matcha ganache 271–2

Pandan Swiss roll with coconut jam 260
    Raspberry jelly cakes 224
    Val's Vietnamese honeycomb cake (bánh bò nướng) 250
Cantonese stir-fried tomato & egg 104
capsicum
    Asian slaw 193–4
    Jono's bacon & pineapple fried rice 93
    Maria's chargrilled veg & pesto on fresh lepinji 53
    Tamarind prawns 84
caramel 218
caramel, balsamic 274
carrots
    Afghan-style rice with cauliflower or chicken 202
    Asian slaw 193–4
    Avgolemono 60
    carrots & currants 202
    Joëlle's oeufs en meurette 178
    Margaret's curry cashew slaw 146
carrots & currants 202
cashew nuts: Margaret's curry cashew slaw 146
Cassie Lee's no-cook tomato sauce 24
cauliflower
    Afghan-style rice with cauliflower or chicken 202
    Not-boring roasted broccoli & sweet potato 22
    Roasted cauli, gruyere sauce, hazelnuts, crispy kale & poachies 168
Cavatelli with anchovy butter & fresh tomato 167
celery
    Avgolemono 60
    Joëlle's oeufs en meurette 178
    prawn stock 177
chai, My 217
cheese
    Brazilian cheese bread (pão de queijo) 40
    Grilled chicken tortillas with charred corn, kiwi salsa & jalapeno cream 208
    No-cook puttanesca with spaghettini 96
    pesto 53
    Roasted cauli, gruyere sauce, hazelnuts, crispy kale & poachies 168
    Sardinian culurgiòne with burnt sage butter 122
    Sourdough fruit loaf, prosciutto, honey & cheese 56

Strawberries, mascarpone yoghurt cream & balsamic caramel 274
Summer pea & mint risotto 188
Tomato, burrata, anchovies & balsamic 48

chicken
Afghan-style rice with cauliflower or chicken 202
Avgolemono 60
Chicken, long bean & preserved olive stir-fry 90
Coconut chicken congee with lime 68
Fast butter chicken 158
Grilled chicken tortillas with charred corn, kiwi salsa & jalapeno cream 208
Korean-style 5-minute spicy chicken with sesame-pickled cukes 88
Pork & kimchi dumplings with Thai chilli jam 126
Steamed ginger chicken with lapcheong & shiitake mushrooms 82
Thyme, lemon & garlic chicken with pan-fried potatoes 148

chickpeas: Hummus 205

chillies
Chilli-hoisin caramel apple cake 218
Coconut chicken congee with lime 68
Cold vegetarian dan dan noodles 130–1
Fast pho 70
green apple & chilli relish 160
jalapeño cream 208
khmer kroeung spice paste 193–4
Korean-style 5-minute spicy chicken with sesame-pickled cukes 88
Mapo tofu 64
No-cook puttanesca with spaghettini 96
Pork & kimchi dumplings with Thai chilli jam 126
salad dressing 193–4
sambal 109
spicy pickled radish 72
Sreymom's Cambodian fish amok with coconut rice & Asian slaw 193–4
Szechuan chilli oil 130–1

Chinese broccoli see gai lan
chips, Crispy nori 37
chocolate: Lychee chiffon cake with white chocolate matcha ganache 271–2

choy sum
Cold vegetarian dan dan noodles 130–1
Meltdown ramen 28
Sesame omelette soup with rice vermicelli 63

Cinnamon doughnut drops 236
Classic vanilla custard tart 242
cleaning tips 27, 67, 79, 137

coconut
6-minute microwave kaya – Malaysian coconut jam 257
Coconut chicken congee with lime 68

Coconut rice pudding with jackfruit & lychees 246
Comforting kale, coconut & beetroot curry 76
Hawaiian butter mochi cake 254
Lychee chiffon cake with white chocolate matcha ganache 271–2
Pandan Swiss roll with coconut jam 260
Prawn & pork balls, glass vermicelli in fragrant coconut sauce 156
Raspberry jelly cakes 224
Sreymom's Cambodian fish amok with coconut rice & Asian slaw 193–4
Teena's Vietnamese sweet mung bean & coconut soup (lek tau suan) 248
Val's Vietnamese honeycomb cake (bánh bò nướng) 250

Cold vegetarian dan dan noodles 130–1
Comforting kale, coconut & beetroot curry 76
compote, strawberry 268

congee
Coconut chicken congee with lime 68
oyster congee 72

cookies
Gingerbreads & how to ice them well 229
Sarah's super-peanutty peanut cookies 223

corn: Grilled chicken tortillas with charred corn, kiwi salsa & jalapeno cream 208

creams
jalapeño cream 208
lychee cream 271–2
mascarpone yoghurt cream 274
peanut butter cream 223
raspberry cream 224
strawberry cream 268
vanilla sour cream 235

Crepes, maple syrup & vanilla ice cream (aka uni special) 238
Crispy nori chips 37
crispy salmon skin 100

cucumbers
Fattoush 205
Fish-fragrant eggplant & bashed cucumber salad 198
Hand-rolled sushi 138
Mum's Malaysian sambal lemak with leftover rice, fried eggs & cucumber 109
raita 158
Sesame-pickled cucumbers 46

culurgiòne, Sardinian, with burnt sage butter 122

curries
Comforting kale, coconut & beetroot curry 76
Fast butter chicken 158

curry mayo dressing 146
custard 265
custard, splitting 253
custard, using the microwave 252

D
dijon–lemon dressing 20
dill dressing 213

dips
Babaganoush 204
Hummus 205
Life-changing guacamole 34

Dirt & dandelions 151–3
doughnut drops, Cinnamon 236

dressings 130–1, 205
curry mayo dressing 146
dijon–lemon dressing 20
dill dressing 213
honey–balsamic dressing 20
salad dressing 193–4

dumpling dough 122
dumpling skins 126

dumplings
Pork & kimchi dumplings with Thai chilli jam 126
Thai-style sago dumplings with sweet pepper pork in lettuce cups 196

E
Easy sweet soy pork with oyster congee & spicy pickled radishes 72–3

eggplant
Babaganoush 204
Fish-fragrant eggplant & bashed cucumber salad 198
Maria's chargrilled veg & pesto on fresh lepinji 53
Xar's charred eggplant omelette 105

eggs
Asparagus, hollandaise, eggs & ham 180–1
Avgolemono 60
Cantonese stir-fried tomato & egg 104
Classic vanilla custard tart 242
Floating islands (île flottante) 265–6
Great Aunty Kim's mint omelette 104
Joélle's oeufs en meurette 178
Jono's bacon & pineapple fried rice 93
Meltdown ramen 28
Mum's Malaysian sambal lemak with leftover rice, fried eggs & cucumber 109
Roasted cauli, gruyere sauce, hazelnuts, crispy kale & poachies 168
Scandi-style smoked salmon, potato & boiled egg salad 213
Sesame omelette soup with rice vermicelli 63
Spam omelette sandwiches 45
Vegetarian chawanmushi with shiitake & konyakku bundles 142
Xar's charred eggplant omelette 105

Enoki, garlic scapes & malt vinegar sauce 98

F

Fast butter chicken 158
Fast pho 70
Fattoush 205
fennel
    prawn stock 177
    T-bone steak with bagna cauda & charred fennel 171
Fermented bean curd & lettuce stir-fry 111
fish
    Flathead with burnt butter, lemon & caper sauce 118
    Meltdown ramen 28
    Sreymom's Cambodian fish amok with coconut rice & Asian slaw 193–4
    White fish with miso beurre blanc, salmon roe & green salad 163
    see also anchovies, salmon
Fish-fragrant eggplant & bashed cucumber salad 198
Flathead with burnt butter, lemon & caper sauce 118
Floating islands (île flottante) 265–6
fried rice, Jono's bacon & pineapple 93
fruit trees 153

G

gai lan: Steamed ginger chicken with lapcheong & shiitake mushrooms 82
ganache, matcha 271
gardening 113, 151–3
garlic oil 196
Gingerbreads & how to ice them well 229
Great Aunty Kim's mint omelette 104
green apple & chilli relish 160
green beans & almonds 118
green salad 163
Grilled chicken tortillas with charred corn, kiwi salsa & jalapeno cream 208
gruyere sauce 168

H

Hand-rolled sushi 138
Handmade semolina cavatelli 135
handmade wheat noodles 130–1
Hawaiian butter mochi cake 254
hazelnuts: Roasted cauli, gruyere sauce, hazelnuts, crispy kale & poachies 168
hollandaise 108
honey–balsamic dressing 20
Hummus 205

I

icing
    piping tips & tricks 231
    royal icing 229
    tips for icing cakes 258
Israeli pita 204

J

jackfruit: Coconut rice pudding with jackfruit & lychees 246
jalapeño cream 208
jam, 6-minute microwave kaya – Malaysian coconut 257
jars, sterilising 257
Jerusalem artichoke velouté with truffle oil 186
Joélle's oeufs en meurette 178
Jono's bacon & pineapple fried rice 93

K

kale
    Comforting kale, coconut & beetroot curry 76
    Mixed mushroom & kale stir-fry with nori & lemon 117
    Roasted cauli, gruyere sauce, hazelnuts, crispy kale & poachies 168
kaya, 6-minute microwave – Malaysian coconut jam 257
khmer kroeung spice paste 193–4
Kimchi, fried seaweed, rice 42
kiwi salsa 208
Korean-style 5-minute spicy chicken with sesame-pickled cukes 88

L

leeks: Korean-style 5-minute spicy chicken with sesame-pickled cukes 88
lemons
    Avgolemono 60
    Babaganoush 204
    burnt sage butter 122
    dill dressing 213
    dressing 205
    Flathead with burnt butter, lemon & caper sauce 118
    freezing zest 50
    hollandaise 108
    Hummus 205
    jalapeño cream 208
    Life-changing guacamole 34
    Mixed mushroom & kale stir-fry with nori & lemon 117
    salad dressing 193–4
    Thyme, lemon & garlic chicken with pan-fried potatoes 148
lentils: Comforting kale, coconut & beetroot curry 76
lettuce cups, Thai-style sago dumplings with sweet pepper pork in 196
Life-changing guacamole 34
limes
    Coconut chicken congee with lime 68
    freezing zest 50
    Life-changing guacamole 34
    Prawn & pork balls, glass vermicelli in fragrant coconut sauce 156
    salad dressing 193–4
lychees
    Coconut rice pudding with jackfruit & lychees 246
    Lychee chiffon cake with white chocolate matcha ganache 271–2

M

malt vinegar sauce 98
Mama Yeow's sweet pork buns 124
Mapo tofu 64
Margaret's curry cashew slaw 146
Maria's chargrilled veg & pesto on fresh lepinji 53
mascarpone yoghurt cream 274
matcha ganache 271
Meltdown ramen 28
Mini Israeli-style feast 204–5
mirépoix 178
miso beurre blanc 163
miso sauce 100
Miso-glazed salmon or eggplant with crunchy greens 100
Mixed mushroom & kale stir-fry with nori & lemon 117
Mum's Malaysian sambal lemak with leftover rice, fried eggs & cucumber 109
mushrooms
    Cold vegetarian dan dan noodles 130–1
    Enoki, garlic scapes & malt vinegar sauce 98
    Joélle's oeufs en meurette 178
    Meltdown ramen 28
    mirépoix 178
    Mixed mushroom & kale stir-fry with nori & lemon 117
    Sesame omelette soup with rice vermicelli 63
    Steamed ginger chicken with lapcheong & shiitake mushrooms 82
    Vegetarian chawanmushi with shiitake & konyakku bundles 142
    White fish with miso beurre blanc, salmon roe & green salad 163
My chai 217
My two fave salad dressings: dijon–lemon & honey–balsamic 20

N

No-cook puttanesca with spaghettini 96
noodles
    Cold vegetarian dan dan noodles 130–1
    Fast pho 70
    Prawn & pork balls, glass vermicelli in fragrant coconut sauce 156
    Sesame omelette soup with rice vermicelli 63
    Vegetarian chawanmushi with shiitake & konyakku bundles 142
Not-boring roasted broccoli & sweet potato 22

nuts
  chopping 38
  roasting in the microwave 10
  see also almonds, cashew nuts,
    hazelnuts, peanuts, pine nuts

O

oeufs en meurette, Joélle's 178
oil, garlic 196
olives
  Chicken, long bean & preserved olive
    stir-fry 90
  No-cook puttanesca with
    spaghettini 96
omelettes
  Cantonese stir-fried tomato &
    egg 104
  Great Aunty Kim's mint omelette 104
  Xar's charred eggplant omelette 105
oranges
  Floating islands (île flottante) 265–6
    orange & almond pastry 242, 268
  Strawberries, mascarpone yoghurt
    cream & balsamic caramel 274
oysters: Easy sweet soy pork with oyster
  congee & spicy pickled radishes 72–3

P

pan-fried potatoes 148
pancakes
  Crepes, maple syrup & vanilla ice
    cream (aka uni special) 238
  Pancakes with banana, butterscotch
    sauce & vanilla sour cream 235
pandan
  6-minute microwave kaya – Malaysian
    coconut jam 257
  Coconut rice pudding with jackfruit &
    lychees 246
  Pandan Swiss roll with coconut
    jam 260
  pandan syrup 248
  Teena's Vietnamese sweet mung bean
    & coconut soup (lek tau suan) 248
  Val's Vietnamese honeycomb cake
    (bánh bò nướng) 250
Pão de queijo (Brazilian cheese bread) 40
pasta
  Cavatelli with anchovy butter & fresh
    tomato 167
  Handmade semolina cavatelli 135
  No-cook puttanesca with
    spaghettini 96
  Zen's creamy zucchini & ancho pasta
    sauce 174
paste, anchovy & garlic 167
pastry, orange & almond pastry 242, 268
peanuts
  peanut butter cream 223
  Sarah's super-peanutty peanut
    cookies 223

Sreymom's Cambodian fish amok with
  coconut rice & Asian slaw 193–4
Thai-style sago dumplings with sweet
  pepper pork in lettuce cups 196
pears: Spiced pork chops with charred
  pears 114
peas
  Miso-glazed salmon or eggplant with
    crunchy greens 100
  Prawn & asparagus risotto with burnt
    sage butter 177
  Summer pea & mint risotto 188
pesto 53
pickled radish, spicy 72
pineapple: Jono's bacon & pineapple fried
  rice 93
piping tips & tricks 231
pipis: White fish with miso beurre blanc,
  salmon roe & green salad 163
pita, Israeli 204
planting flowers 152
planting seeds and seedlings 152
pork
  Asparagus, hollandaise, eggs &
    ham 180–1
  Easy sweet soy pork with oyster congee
    & spicy pickled radishes 72–3
  Jono's bacon & pineapple fried rice 93
  Mama Yeow's sweet pork buns 124
  Mapo tofu 64
  Pork & kimchi dumplings with Thai
    chilli jam 126
  Prawn & pork balls, glass vermicelli in
    fragrant coconut sauce 156
  Sesame omelette soup with rice
    vermicelli 63
  Sourdough fruit loaf, prosciutto, honey
    & cheese 56
  Spiced pork chops with charred
    pears 114
  Steamed ginger chicken with lapcheong
    & shiitake mushrooms 82
  Thai-style sago dumplings with sweet
    pepper pork in lettuce cups 196
potatoes
  Afghan-style rice with cauliflower or
    chicken 202
  Joélle's oeufs en meurette 178
  Sardinian culurgiòne with burnt sage
    butter 122
  Scandi-style smoked salmon, potato &
    boiled egg salad 213
  The best roasted smashed potatoes 19
  Thyme, lemon & garlic chicken with
    pan-fried potatoes 148
prawns
  fish amok 193–4
  Hand-rolled sushi 138
  Meltdown ramen 28
  Prawn & asparagus risotto with burnt
    sage butter 177
  Prawn & pork balls, glass vermicelli in
    fragrant coconut sauce 156

prawn stock 177
Prawn wontons with green apple &
  chilli relish 160
Tamarind prawns 84
pudding, Coconut rice with jackfruit &
  lychees 246

R

radishes
  Easy sweet soy pork with oyster congee
    & spicy pickled radishes 72–3
  Fattoush 205
  Scandi-style smoked salmon, potato &
    boiled egg salad 213
raita 158
raspberry cream 224
Raspberry jelly cakes 224
relish, green apple & chilli 160
rice
  Afghan-style rice with cauliflower or
    chicken 202
  Avgolemono 60
  Coconut chicken congee with lime 68
  Coconut rice pudding with jackfruit &
    lychees 246
  cooking perfect stove-top rice 90
  Hand-rolled sushi 138
  Jono's bacon & pineapple fried rice 93
  Kimchi, fried seaweed, rice 42
  Mum's Malaysian sambal lemak
    with leftover rice, fried eggs &
    cucumber 109
  oyster congee 72
  Prawn & asparagus risotto with burnt
    sage butter 177
  Sreymom's Cambodian fish amok with
    coconut rice & Asian slaw 193–4
  Summer pea & mint risotto 188
  turmeric rice 158
risotto
  Prawn & asparagus risotto with burnt
    sage butter 177
  Summer pea & mint risotto 188
Roasted cauli, gruyere sauce, hazelnuts,
  crispy kale & poachies 168
royal icing 229

S

sago: Thai-style sago dumplings with sweet
  pepper pork in lettuce cups 196
salad dressing 193–4
salads
  Asian slaw 193–4
  cucumber salad 198
  Fattoush 205
  green salad 163
  Scandi-style smoked salmon, potato &
    boiled egg salad 213
salmon
  Miso-glazed salmon or eggplant with
    crunchy greens 100

perfect crispy salmon skin 100
Scandi-style smoked salmon, potato &
boiled egg salad 213
salsa, kiwi 208
sambal 109
sandwiches
Maria's chargrilled veg & pesto on fresh
lepinji 53
Sourdough fruit loaf, prosciutto, honey
& cheese 56
Spam omelette sandwiches 45
Sarah's strawberries & cream tart 268
Sarah's super-peanutty peanut
cookies 223
Sardinian culurgiòne with burnt sage
butter 122
sauces
bagna cauda 171
burnt sage butter 122
butterscotch sauce 235
Cassie Lee's no-cook tomato sauce 24
gruyere sauce 168
hollandaise 108
malt vinegar sauce 98
miso beurre blanc 163
miso sauce 100
pesto 53
sour cream sauce 213
velouté 186
Scandi-style smoked salmon, potato &
boiled egg salad 213
seaweed
Crispy nori chips 37
Hand-rolled sushi 138
Kimchi, fried seaweed, rice 42
Meltdown ramen 28
Mixed mushroom & kale stir-fry with
nori & lemon 117
seeds and seedlings, planting 152
Sesame-pickled cucumbers 46
Sesame omelette soup with rice
vermicelli 63
silver, polishing 78
soups
Avgolemono 60
Fast pho 70
Meltdown ramen 28
Sesame omelette soup with rice
vermicelli 63
Teena's Vietnamese sweet mung bean
& coconut soup (lek tau suan) 248
sour cream sauce 213
Sourdough bread 14–5
Sourdough fruit loaf, prosciutto, honey &
cheese 56
Spam omelette sandwiches 45
spice mixes
cinnamon sugar 236
khmer kroeung spice paste 193–4
Spiced pork chops with charred pears 114
spicy pickled radish 72
spring onions, curly 82

Sreymom's Cambodian fish amok with
coconut rice & Asian slaw 193–4
starter, sourdough 14
Steamed ginger chicken with lapcheong &
shiitake mushrooms 82
sterilising jars 257
stir-fries
Cantonese stir-fried tomato &
egg 104
Chicken, long bean & preserved olive
stir-fry 90
Mixed mushroom & kale stir-fry with
nori & lemon 117
stock, prawn 177
strawberries
Pancakes with banana, butterscotch
sauce & vanilla sour cream 235
Sarah's strawberries & cream tart 268
Strawberries, mascarpone yoghurt
cream & balsamic caramel 274
strawberry compote 268
Summer pea & mint risotto 188
sushi, Hand-rolled 138
sweet soy pork 72
sweet potato: Not-boring roasted broccoli
& sweet potato 22
sweetcorn see corn
Swiss roll, Pandan, with coconut jam 260
syrup, pandan 248
Szechuan chilli oil 130–1

T

T-bone steak with bagna cauda & charred
fennel 171
tamarind
sambal 109
Tamarind prawns 84
tarts
Classic vanilla custard tart 242
Sarah's strawberries & cream tart 268
tea
ginger tea 173
My chai 217
Teena's Vietnamese sweet mung bean &
coconut soup (lek tau suan) 248
Thai-style sago dumplings with sweet
pepper pork in lettuce cups 196
The best roasted smashed potatoes 19
Three omelettes to have with rice 104–5
Thyme, lemon & garlic chicken with
pan-fried potatoes 148
tofu
Fermented bean curd & lettuce
stir-fry 111
Mapo tofu 64
Meltdown ramen 28
tomatoes
Afghan-style rice with cauliflower or
chicken 202
Cantonese stir-fried tomato & egg 104
Cassie Lee's no-cook tomato sauce 24

Cavatelli with anchovy butter & fresh
tomato 167
Fast butter chicken 158
Fattoush 205
Life-changing guacamole 34
No-cook puttanesca with
spaghettini 96
Tomato, burrata, anchovies &
balsamic 48
tortillas, Grilled chicken, with charred corn,
kiwi salsa & jalapeno cream 208
turmeric rice 158

V

Val's Vietnamese honeycomb cake (bánh
bò nướng) 250
vanilla sour cream 235
Vegetarian chawanmushi with shiitake &
konyakku bundles 142
velouté, Jerusalem artichoke, with truffle
oil 186

W

water chestnuts: Teena's Vietnamese sweet
mung bean & coconut soup (lek tau
suan) 248
weeding 152
White fish with miso beurre blanc, salmon
roe & green salad 163
wombok see cabbage
wontons, Prawn, with green apple & chilli
relish 160

X

Xar's charred eggplant omelette 105

Z

Zen's creamy zucchini & ancho pasta
sauce 174
zest, freezing citrus 50
zucchini
Maria's chargrilled veg & pesto on fresh
lepinji 53
Zen's creamy zucchini & ancho pasta
sauce 174

Pan Macmillan acknowledges the Traditional Custodians of country throughout Australia and their connections to lands, waters and communities. We pay our respect to Elders past and present and extend that respect to all Aboriginal and Torres Strait Islander peoples today. We honour more than sixty thousand years of storytelling, art and culture.

A Plum book

First published in 2022 by
Pan Macmillan Australia Pty Limited
Level 25, 1 Market Street,
Sydney, NSW 2000, Australia

Level 3, 112 Wellington Parade,
East Melbourne, VIC 3002, Australia

Text copyright © Poh Ling Yeow 2022
Design Kirby Armstrong copyright © Pan Macmillan 2022
Photographs Henry Trumble copyright © Pan Macmillan 2022, except for images on pages 7, 26, 31, 39, 58, 66, 80, 94, 102, 112, 128, 136, 150, 154, 172, 184, 195, 220 and 259 by Gretl Watson-Blazewicz © Pan Macmillan 2022
Illustrations © Sarah Rich 2022

The moral right of the author has been asserted.

Design and typesetting by Kirby Armstrong
Illustration by Sarah Rich
Editing by Ariana Klepac
Index by Helena Holmgren
Photography by Henry Trumble, with additional photography by Gretl Watson-Blazewicz
Prop and food styling by Poh Ling Yeow
Food preparation by Poh Ling Yeow and Mandy Hall
Colour reproduction by Splitting Image Colour Studio
Printed and bound in China by 1010 Printing International Limited

A CIP catalogue record for this book is available from the National Library of Australia.

10 9 8 7 6 5 4 3 2 1